HISTORIC PHOTOS OF
PORTLAND

TEXT AND CAPTIONS BY DONALD R. NELSON

Turner®
Publishing Company
Nashville, Tennessee • Paducah, Kentucky

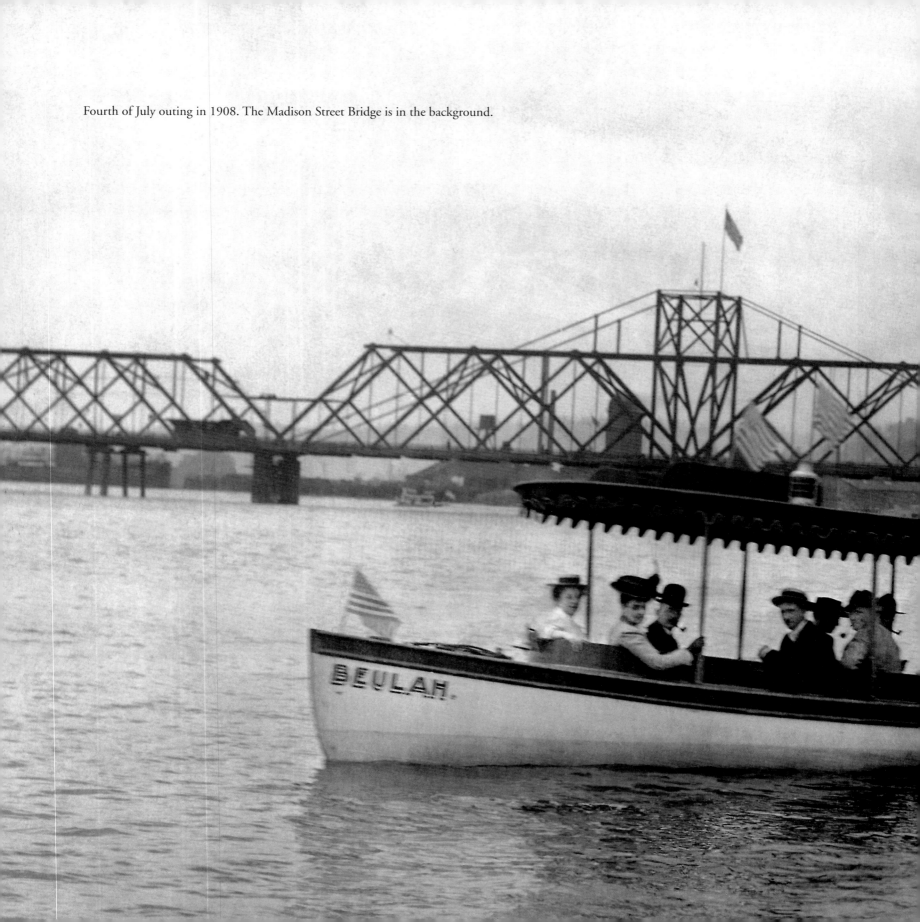

Fourth of July outing in 1908. The Madison Street Bridge is in the background.

HISTORIC PHOTOS OF
PORTLAND

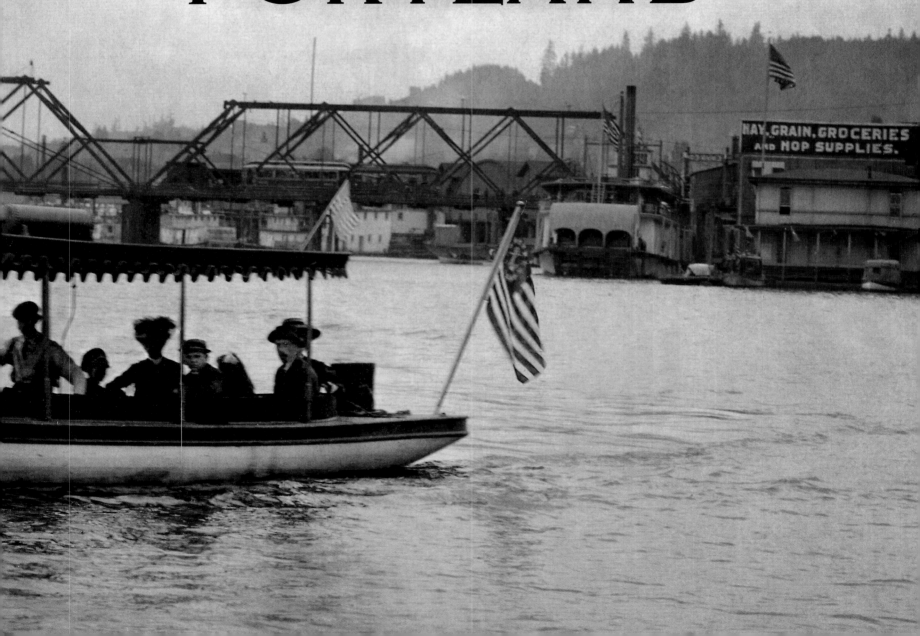

Turner Publishing Company

200 4th Avenue North • Suite 950   412 Broadway • P.O. Box 3101
Nashville, Tennessee 37219   Paducah, Kentucky 42002-3101
(615) 255-2665   (270) 443-0121

www.turnerpublishing.com

Library of Congress Control Number: 2006933651

ISBN: 1-59652-304-2

Printed in the United States of America

0 9 8 7 6 5 4 3 2 1

CONTENTS

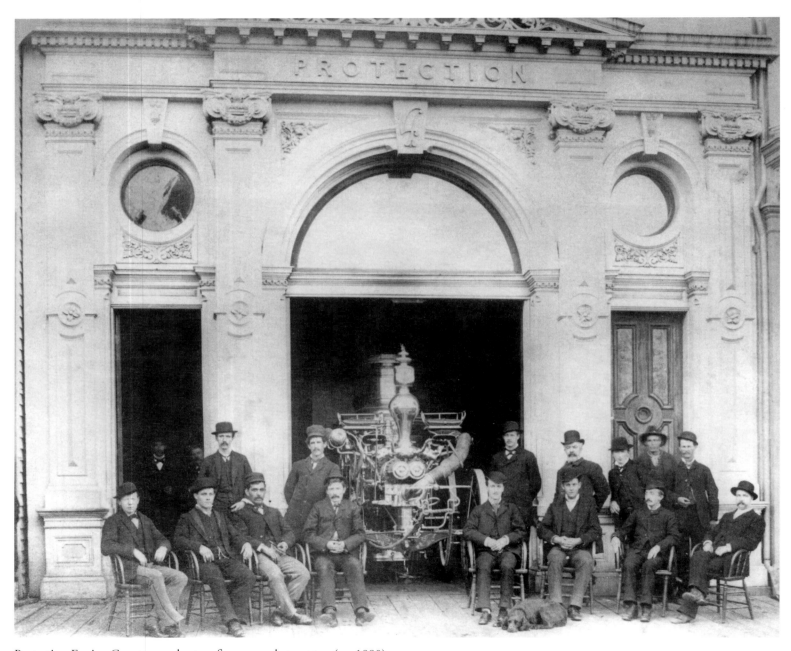

Protection Engine Company volunteer firemen and apparatus (ca. 1880)

Acknowledgments

This volume, *Historic Photos of Portland,* is the result of the cooperation of many individuals, organizations, institutions, and corporations. It is with great thanks that we acknowledge the valuable contribution of the following for their generous support:

City of Portland Archives

Heathman Hotel

Portland Police Historical Society

We would also like to thank the following individuals for their valuable contribution and assistance in making this work possible:

Bill Failing

Tim Hills–McMenamins Pub

Brian Johnson, Assistant Archivist, City of Portland Archives

Lori Kuechler, Executive Director, Portland Police Historical Society

And finally, we would like to thank those who contributed photographs from the following archives:

Mary Couch Robertson Butler Collection

Failing Family Archives

Gholston Collection

Frank Howatt

Nelson Photo Archive

Elaine Wiley

Yamhill County Historical Society

PREFACE

Portland, Oregon, has thousands of historic photographs that reside in archives, both locally and nationally. This book began with the observation that, while those photographs are of great interest to many, they are not easily accessible. During a time when Portland is looking ahead and evaluating its future course, many people are asking, "How do we treat the past?" These decisions affect every aspect of the city—architecture, public spaces, commerce, and infrastructure—and these, in turn, affect the way that people live their lives. This book seeks to provide easy access to a valuable, objective look into Portland's history.

The power of photographs is that they are less subjective than text in their treatment of history. Although the photographer can make decisions regarding subject matter and how to capture and present it, photographs do not provide the breadth of interpretation that text does. For this reason, they offer an original, untainted perspective that allows the viewer to interpret and observe.

This project represents countless hours of review and research. The researchers and author have reviewed thousands of photographs in numerous archives. We greatly appreciate the generous assistance of the archivists listed in the acknowledgments of this work, without whom this project could not have been completed.

The goal in publishing this work is to provide broader access to sets of extraordinary photographs that seek to inspire, provide perspective, and evoke insight that might assist people who are responsible for determining Portland's future. In addition, the book seeks to preserve the past with adequate respect and reverence.

The photographs selected have been reproduced in black and white to provide depth to the images. With the exception of touching up imperfections caused by the damage of time, no other changes have been made. The focus and clarity of many images is limited to the technology and the ability of the photographer at the time they were taken.

The work is divided into eras. Beginning with some of the earliest known photographs of Portland, the first section records photographs from before the Civil War through the end of the nineteenth century. The second section spans the beginning of the twentieth century to World War I. SectionThree moves from World War I to World War II. Finally, Section Four covers World War II to the late 1970s.

In each of these sections we have made an effort to capture various aspects of life through our selection of photographs. People, commerce, transportation, infrastructure, religious institutions, and educational institutions have been included to provide a broad perspective.

We encourage readers to reflect as they walk in front of the Skidmore Fountain, along the Vera Katz Eastbank Esplanade, through Governor Tom McCall Waterfront Park, or through Washington Park. It is the publisher's hope that in utilizing this work, longtime residents will learn something new and that new residents will gain a perspective on where Portland has been, so that each can contribute to its future.

Todd Bottorff, Publisher

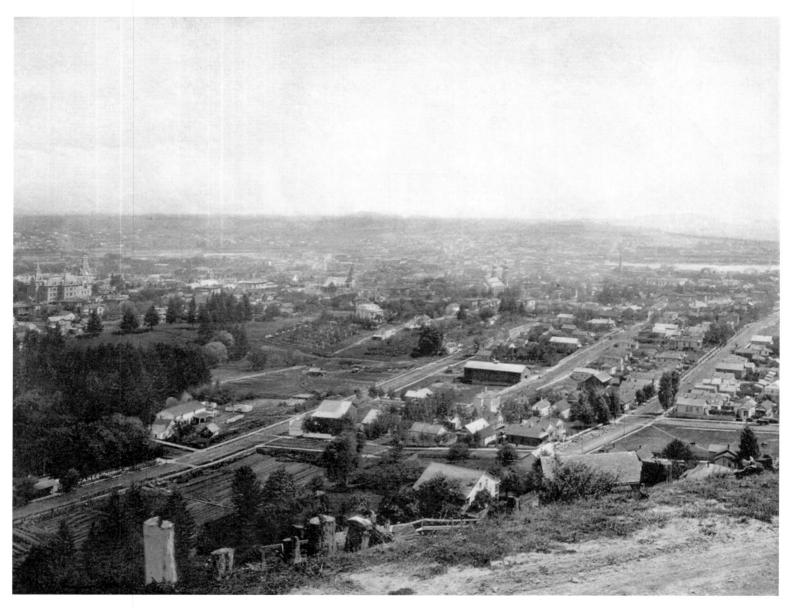

This 1894 panorama shows Goose Hollow on the right. The farm and residence of pioneer steamboat man Jacob Kamm is shown at left-center.

PRE-CIVIL WAR TO THE
END OF THE NINETEENTH CENTURY

1860–1899

Portland, its name determined by a coin toss by two town-site owners, was incorporated in 1851. As the city took shape and began to prosper, the log cabins and frame structures of businesses were replaced by brick and stone buildings. Wood frame churches and synagogues were replaced with larger edifices. Early industries included fishing, lumber, salmon canning, grain and flour milling.

Steam navigation developed in the 1850s. The railroads followed in the 1870s. Public transportation was established in 1872 with horse-drawn streetcars, later usurped by steam and electric conveyances. In 1887, the Morrison Bridge, the city's first bridge, connected Portland to East Portland. Prior to this, ferryboats provided access to the east bank city.

Portland's significance continued to grow. The combined United States Post Office, Courthouse, and Customs House was completed in 1875. The Marquam Grand Opera House and its connected business block opened in 1890. The Portland Hotel was also completed in 1890. The Dekum Building, the Oregonian Building, and the Chamber of Commerce building were all built in 1892.

The cities of East Portland, on the east bank of the Willamette, and Albina to its north were consolidated with the City of Portland in 1891. By 1893, the Library Association of Portland was in its own building; upstairs in the same structure was the Portland Art Museum. Union station was opened in 1896.

Through fires, floods, and hard economic times, the city persevered to grow from a small frontier village into a thriving metropolitan area.

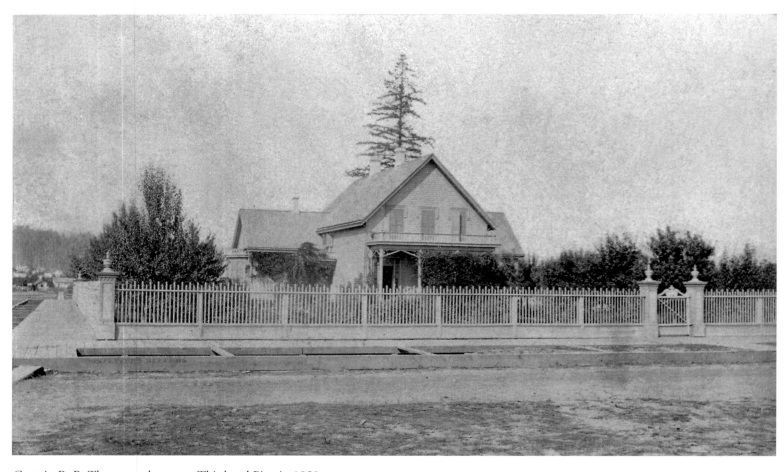

Captain R. R. Thompson house on Third and Pine in 1859

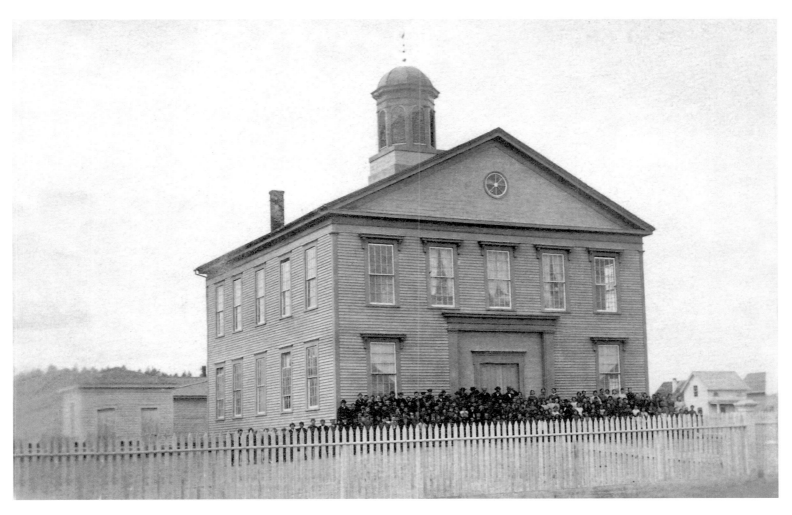

Students pose in front of Central School on Sixth Street in 1865. The school was built in 1858.

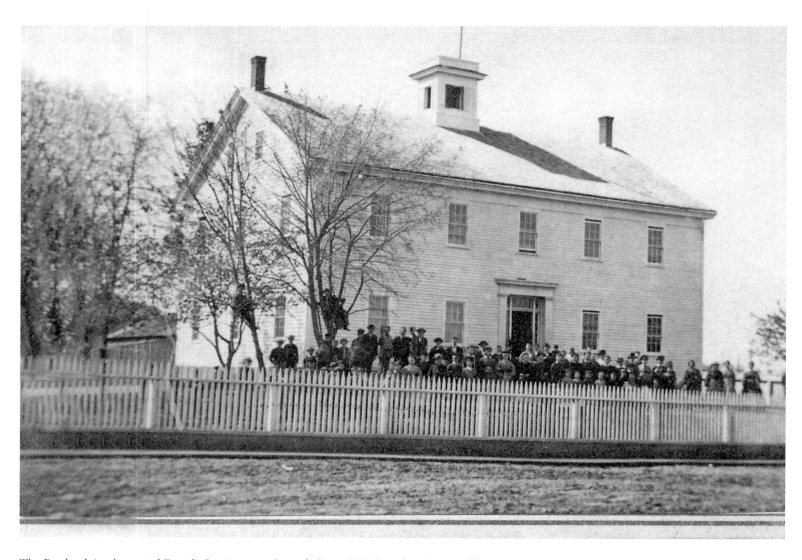

The Portland Academy and Female Seminary on Seventh Street (SW Broadway) near Jefferson, a private Methodist school, built in 1851 is shown in this 1865 view. Unable to compete with public education, the school closed in 1878.

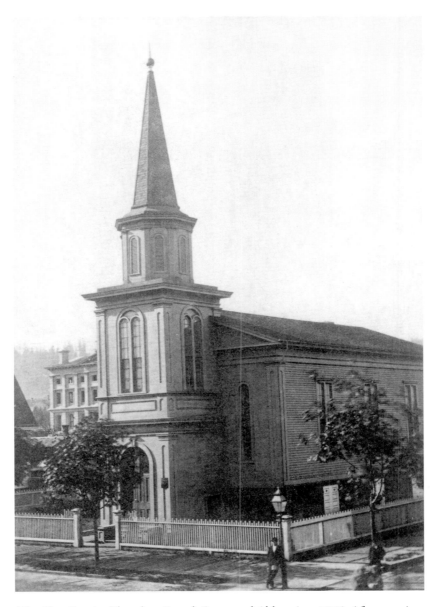

The First Baptist Church at Fourth Street and Alder, circa 1875. After meeting in the basement for eight years, the rest of the structure was completed in 1870.

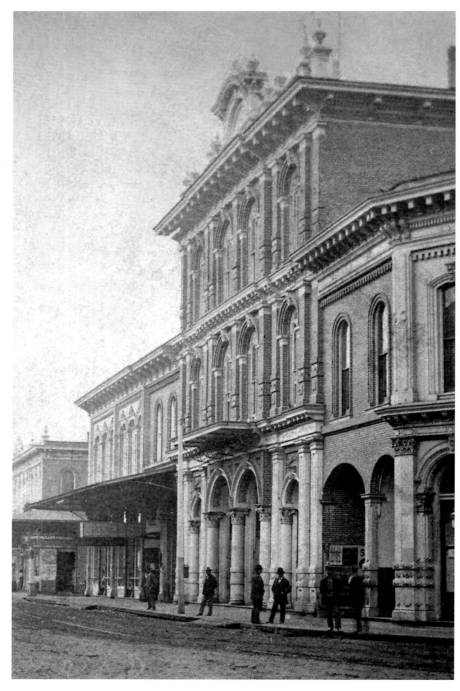

New Market Theatre, circa 1875. The ground floor of the theater
building on First Street contained market spaces where groceries,
dairy products, and a variety of meats were offered.

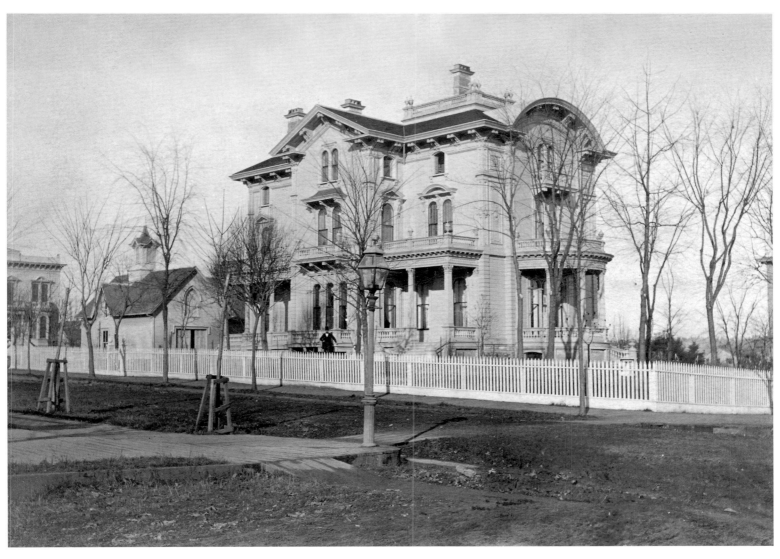

Residence of former United States Senator and pioneer merchant,
Henry W. Corbett, on Fifth and Taylor

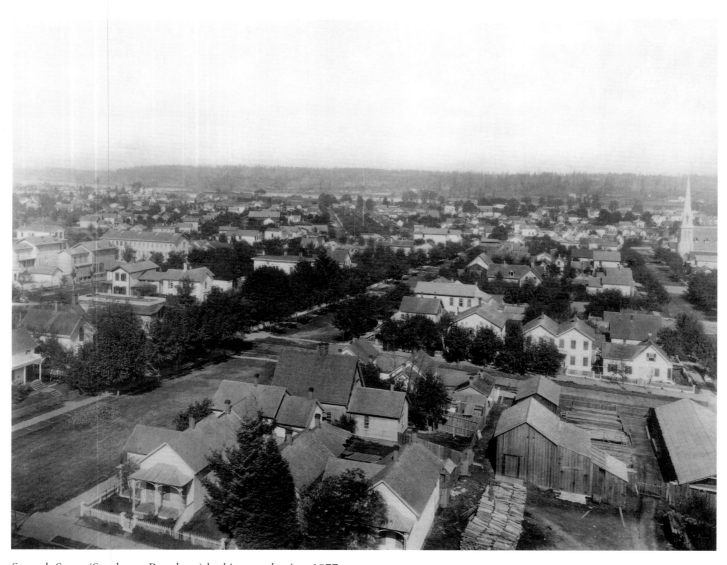

Seventh Street (Southwest Broadway) looking north, circa 1877

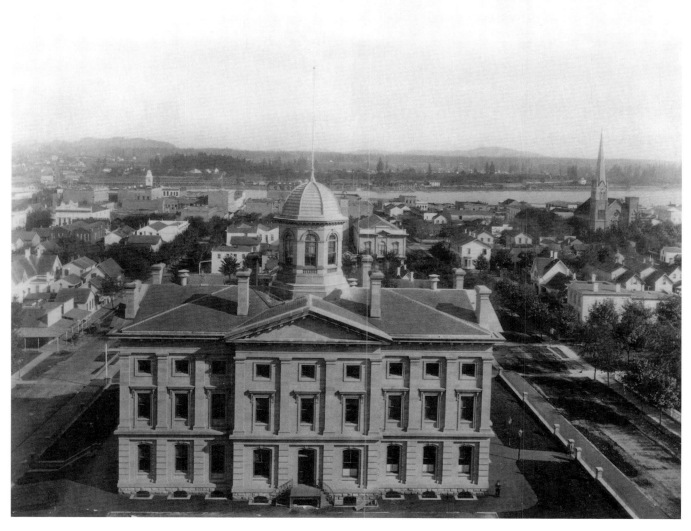

Looking east from the Central School to the Portland Post Office, circa 1877.
The Willamette River is seen in the distance.

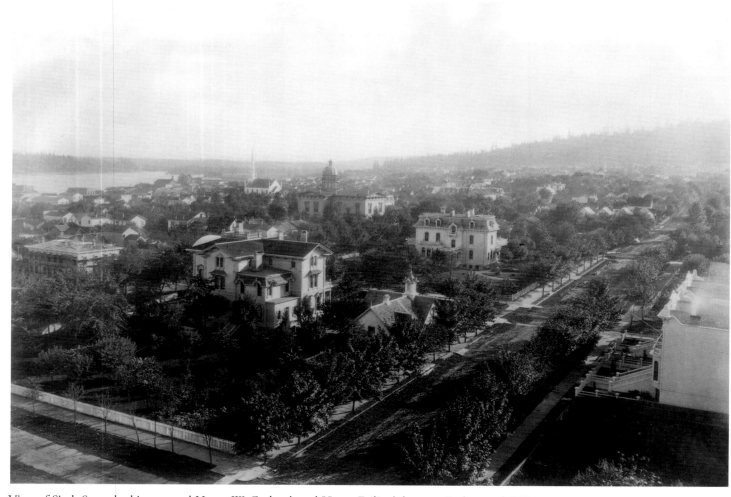

View of Sixth Street looking toward Henry W. Corbett's and Henry Failing's homes. Corbett and Failing were business partners in the wholesale hardware company—Corbett, Failing and Company, circa 1877.

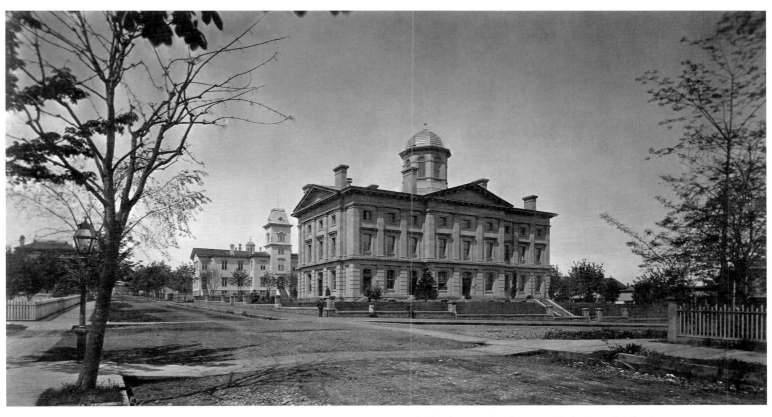

Portland's combined Courthouse, Post Office, and Customs House in 1878. In the background is the expanded Central School.

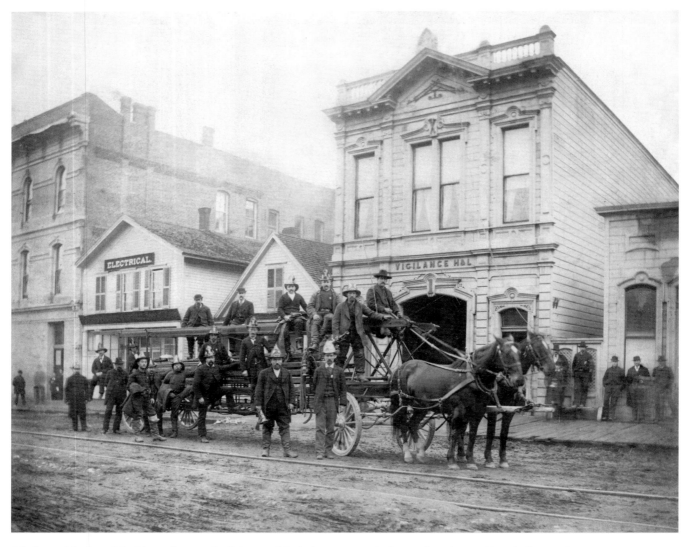

Vigilance Hook and Ladder volunteer firefighters with their apparatus in front of station on Fourth Street, circa 1880

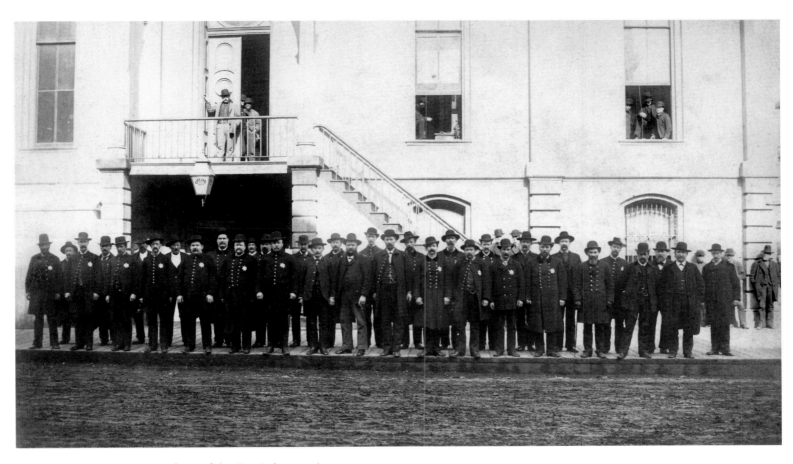

Portland Police force posed in front of the City Jail in 1884

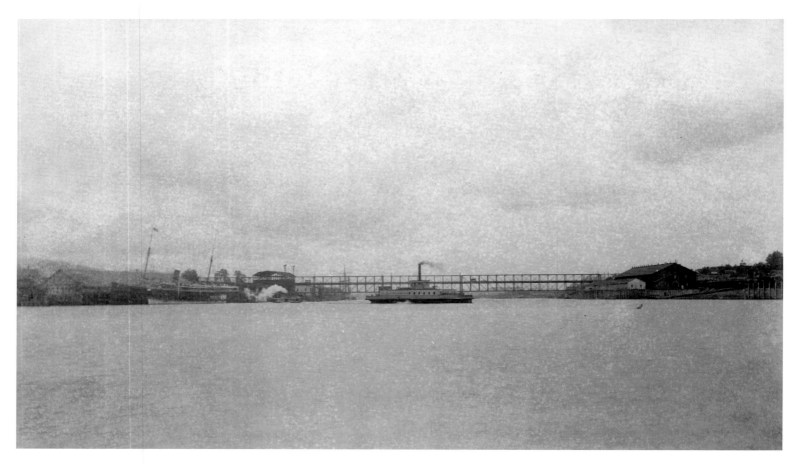

A ferryboat crosses the Willamette River. In the background is the Steel Bridge; the lower level was for railroad traffic, while the upper level was for pedestrian traffic and horse-drawn wagons and carriages, circa 1889.

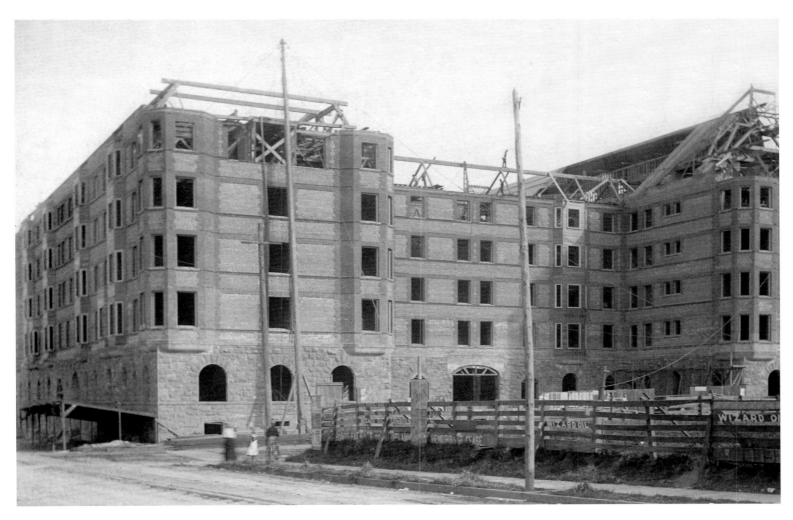

The Portland Hotel, which opened in 1890, was to be built by Henry Villard, President of the Northern Pacific Railroad. Construction was halted in 1884 when financial difficulties arose. Portland businessmen banded together in 1888 to finance its completion. This construction view is from circa 1889, and shows the Seventh Street (Southwest Broadway) side of the hotel.

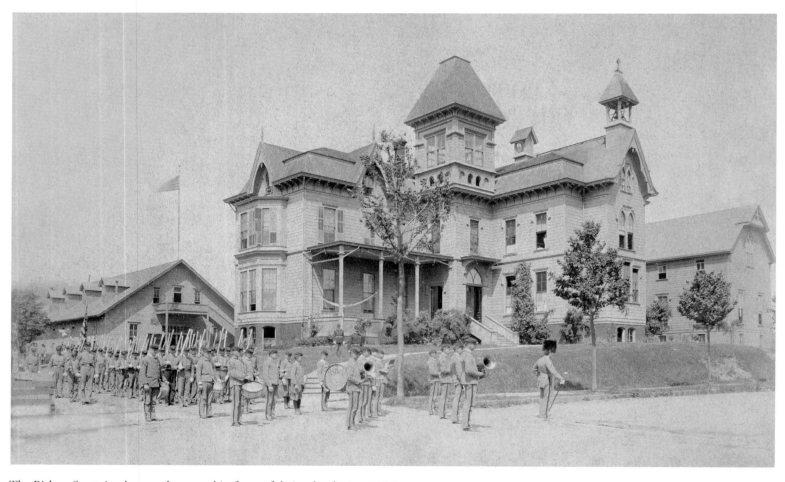

The Bishop Scott Academy cadets posed in front of their school, circa 1890.
The school was named for early Oregon Episcopal Bishop, Thomas Fielding Scott.

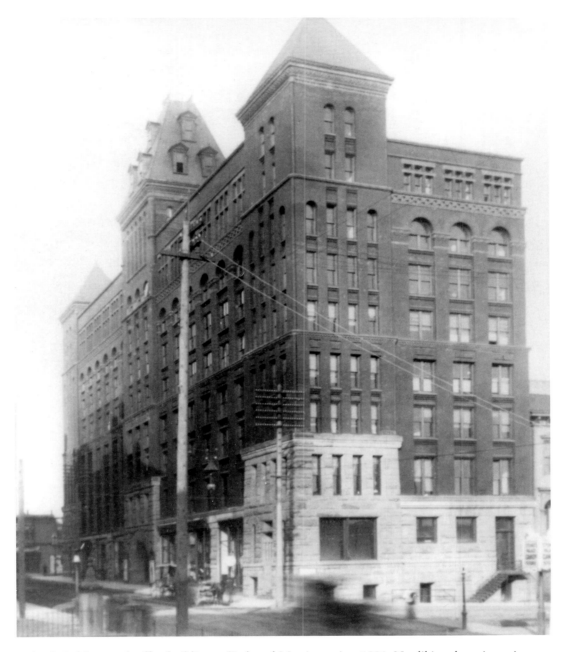

Judge P. A. Marquam's office building at Sixth and Morrison, circa 1890. Not liking the going price for brick, Marquam started his own brickyard to supply material for his structure. The building was dismantled after a wall collapsed in 1912, exposing more structural flaws during renovation for the Northwestern National Bank.

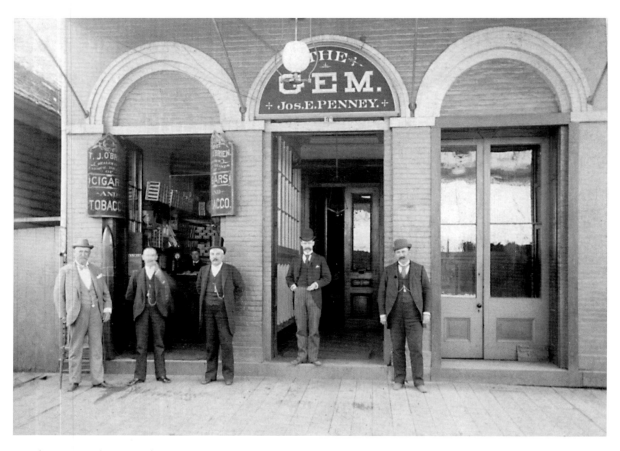

Joseph E. Penney's Gem Saloon on First Street in 1890 was a popular lunch spot for Portland businessmen. Adjoining the Gem was the cigar store of T. J. O'Brien.

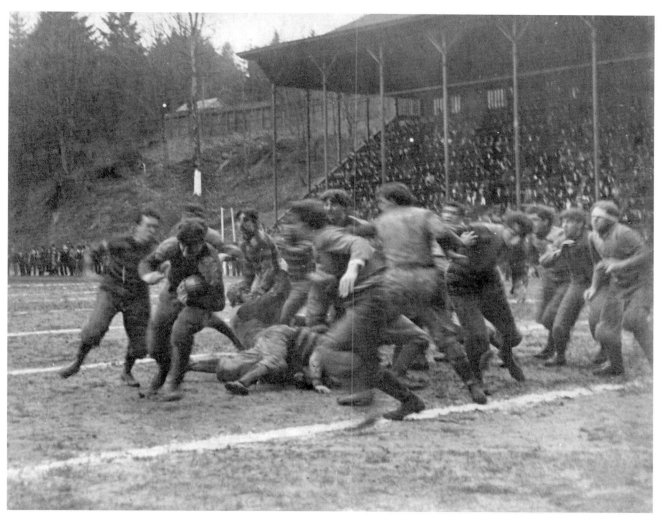

Multnomah Amateur Athletic Club football game at the Multnomah Field in the late 1890s.
The players did not wear helmets at the time.

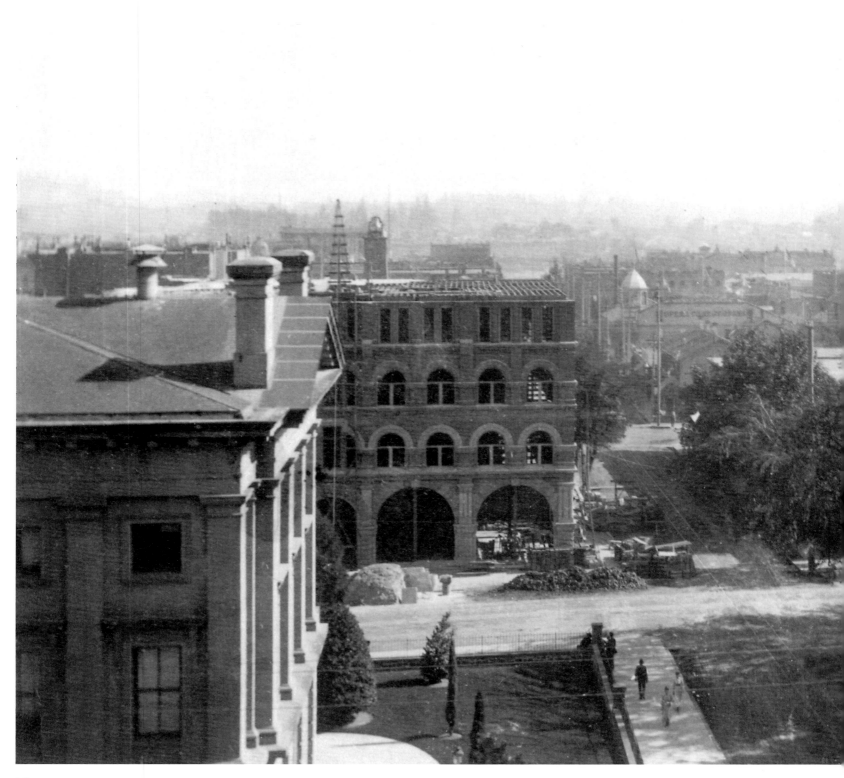

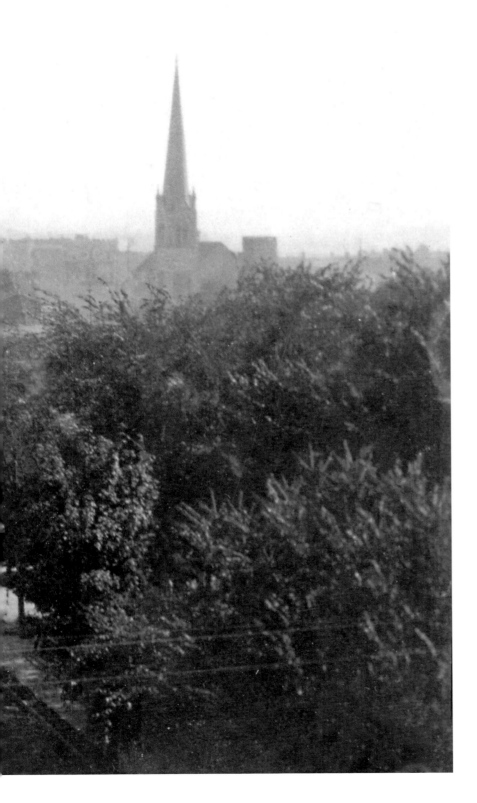

Fifth Street from the Portland Hotel, circa 1891. On the left is the Post Office, the Goodnough Building is under construction, and in the right background is the Taylor Street Methodist Episcopal Church.

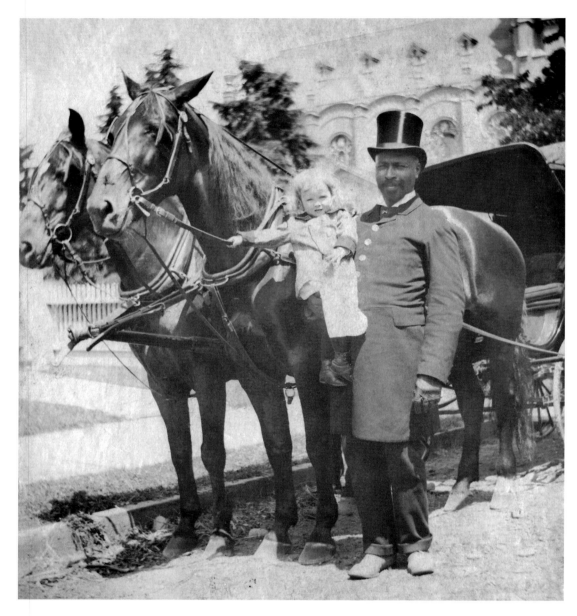

George E. Singleton, coachman for Mr. and Mrs. Henry W. Corbett, holds Mary Corbett Robertson, a grand niece of the Corbetts, circa 1894. Singleton continued employment as a handyman for Mrs. Corbett after an automobile replaced the Corbett's horse-drawn carriages around 1916.

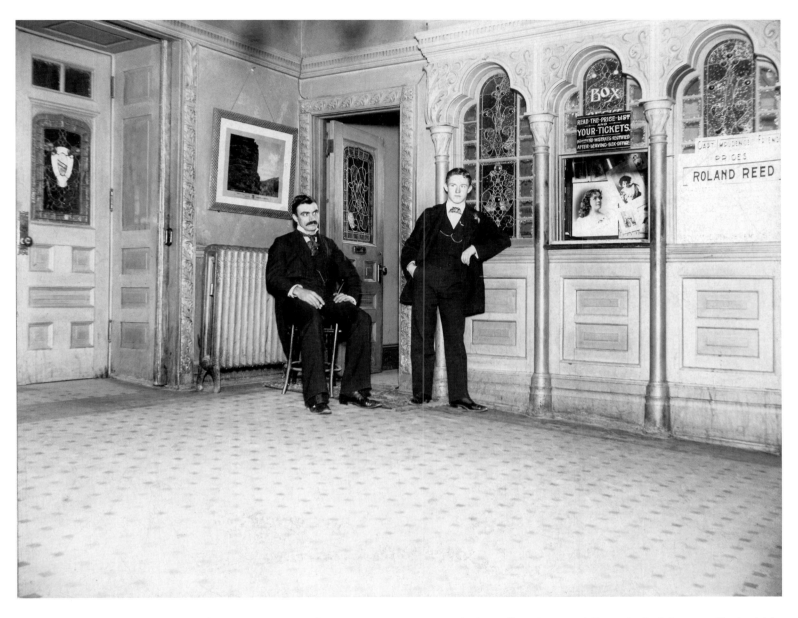

George L. Baker, assistant manager of the Marquam Grand Opera House, sits next to the box office, circa 1896. It was in the Marquam Block which was connected to the theater building. George L. Baker was Portland's mayor from 1917 to 1933.

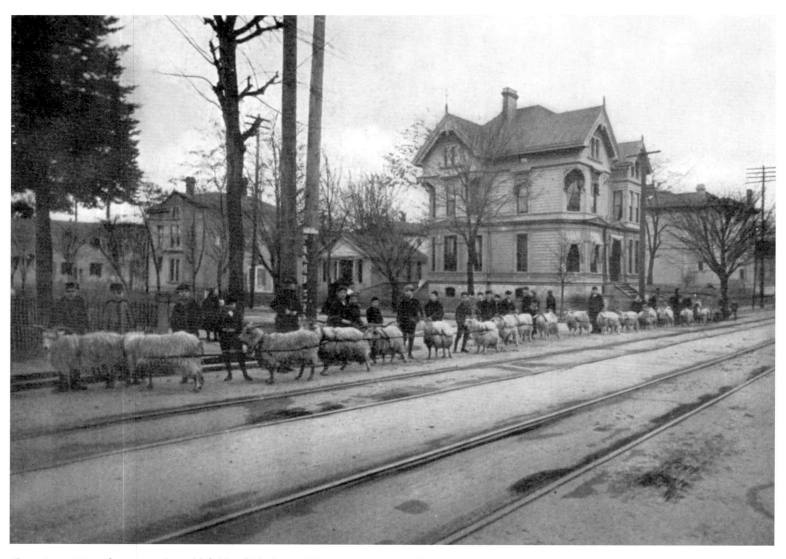

Goats in training, for use on the gold fields of Alaska, on Morrison Street circa late 1890s.

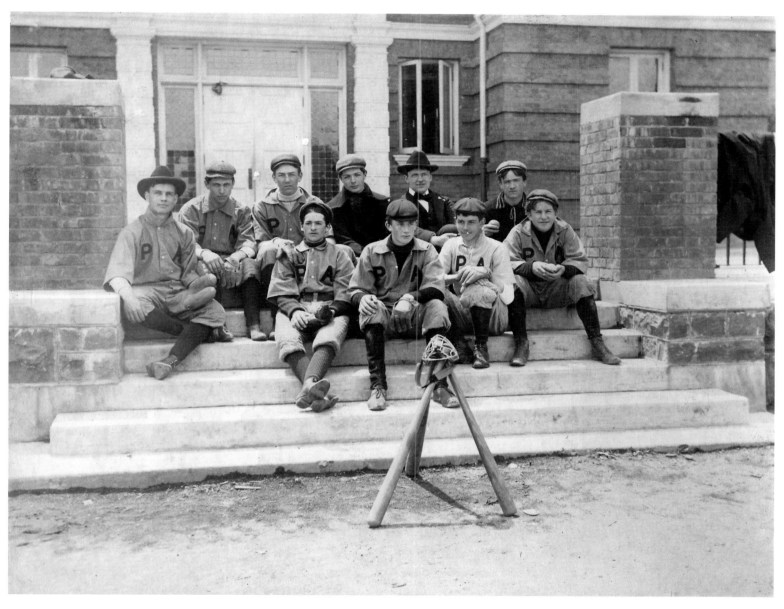

Baseball team of the Portland Academy, circa 1896

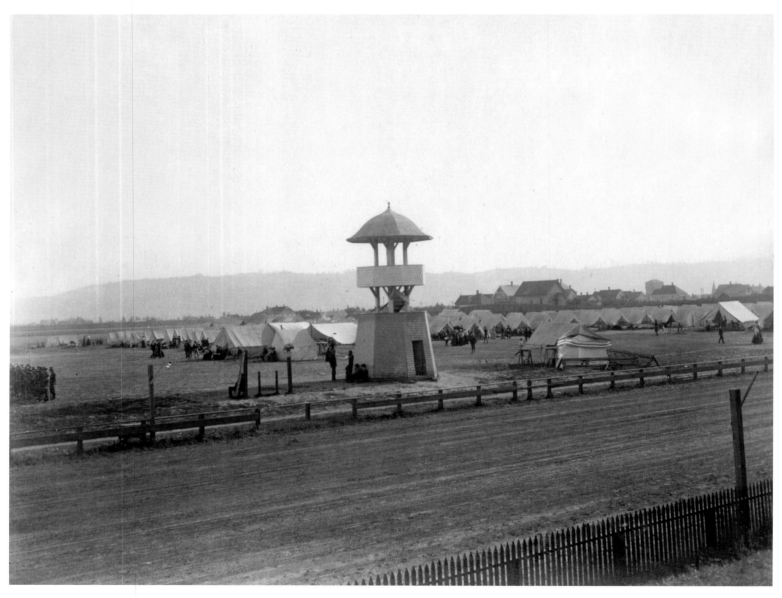

Encampment of Oregon National Guard soldiers at Irvington Race Track awaiting evaluation before becoming part of the Second Oregon Volunteers regiment that went to the Philippines in the Spanish American War, 1898

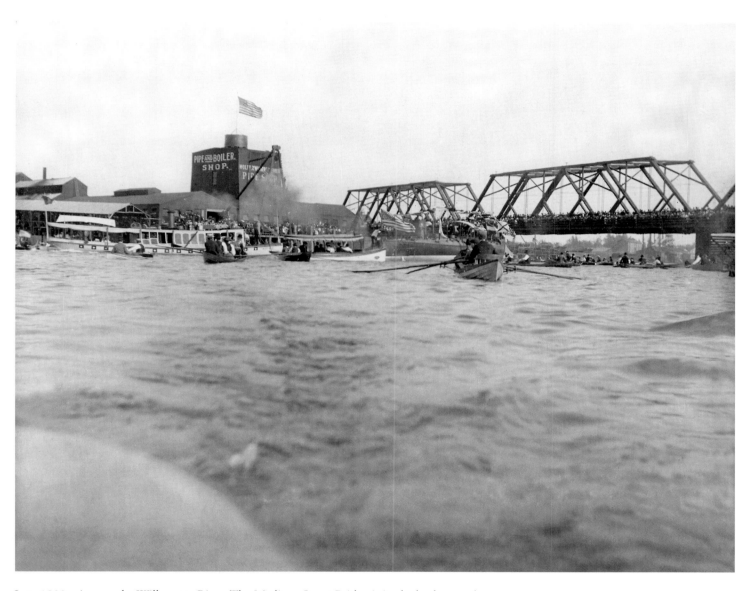

Late 1890s view on the Willamette River. The Madison Street Bridge is in the background.

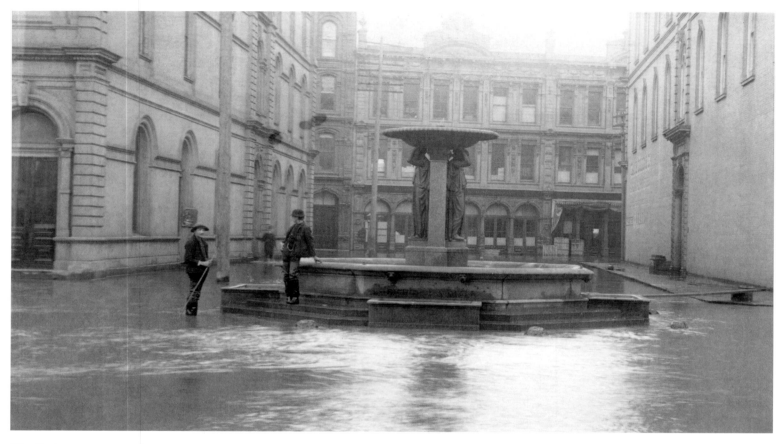

The Skidmore Fountain during the 1890 flood. Completed in 1888, it was built from a $5,000 bequest from pioneer druggist Stephen G. Skidmore and the donations of others. The fountain was for horses and dogs; cups attached by chain to the fountain were for thirsty citizens. Etched on one side of the basin is the phrase "Good Citizens Are The Riches Of A City."

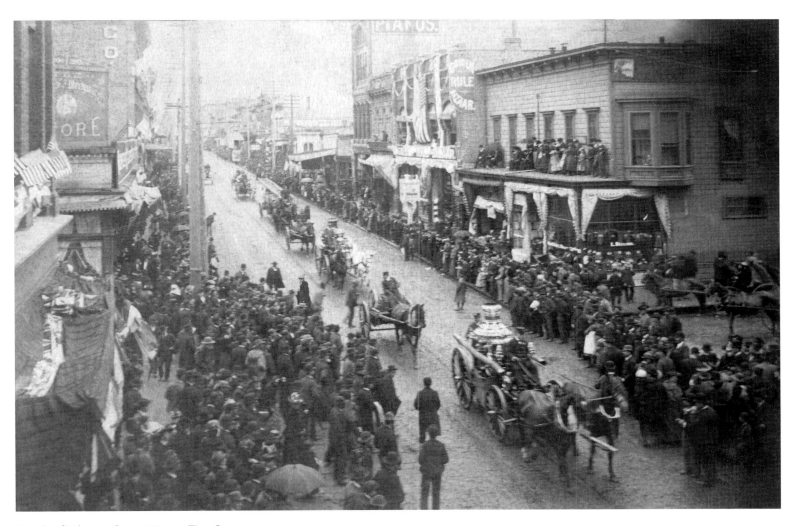

Fourth of July parade in 1891 on First Street

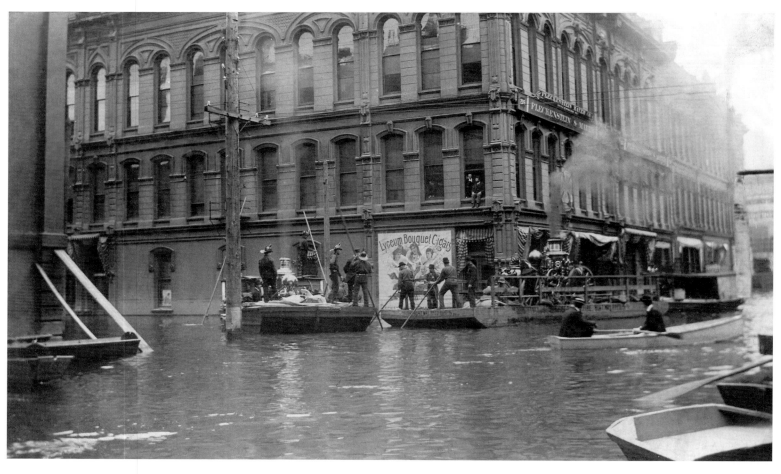

Fire engine on barge at the northeast corner of Second and Oak streets during flood of June 1894

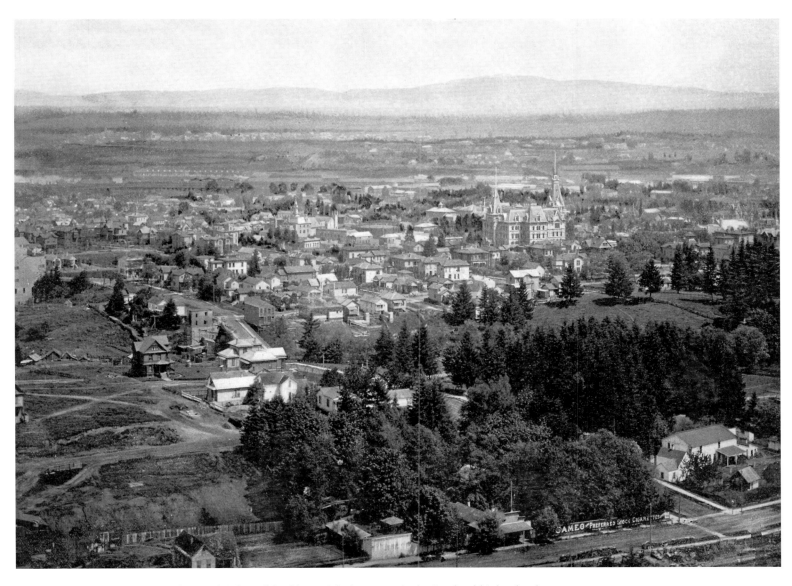

An 1894 panorama looking to the north. The tall building with the towers is the Portland high school.

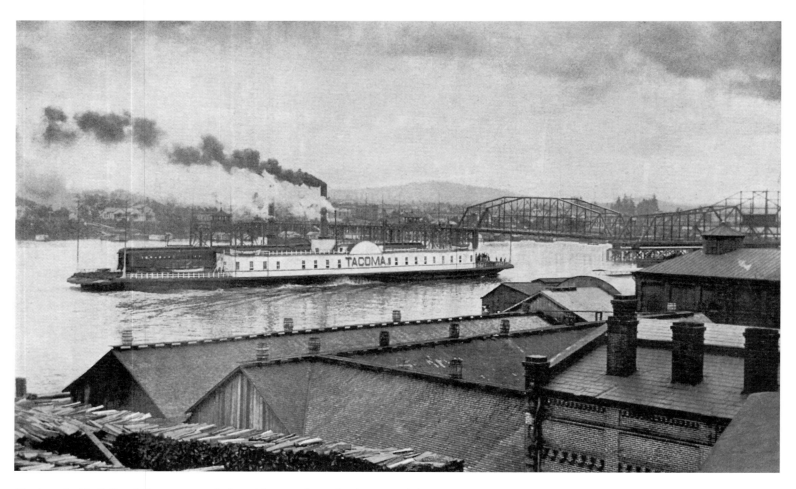

Northern Pacific Railroad Company transfer boat *Tacoma* is shown heading toward the Burnside Bridge to its destination at the Jefferson Street wharf during the 1894 flood. The Portland Gas Company is on the lower right.

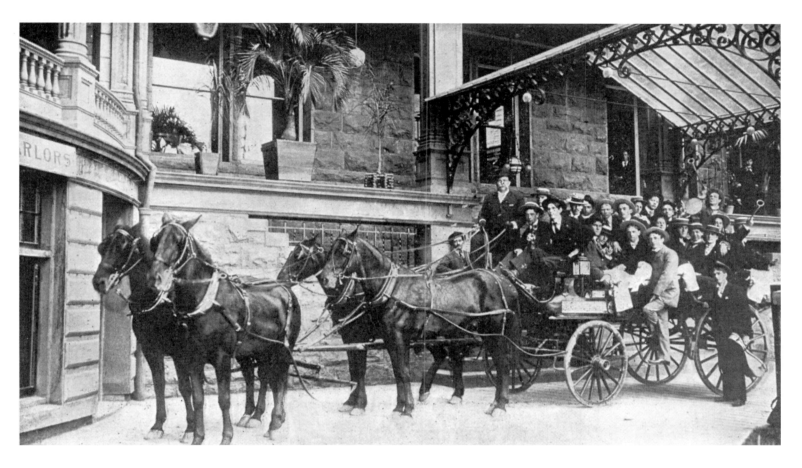

A coaching party, ready for a ride, poses at the entrance to the Portland Hotel in 1896.

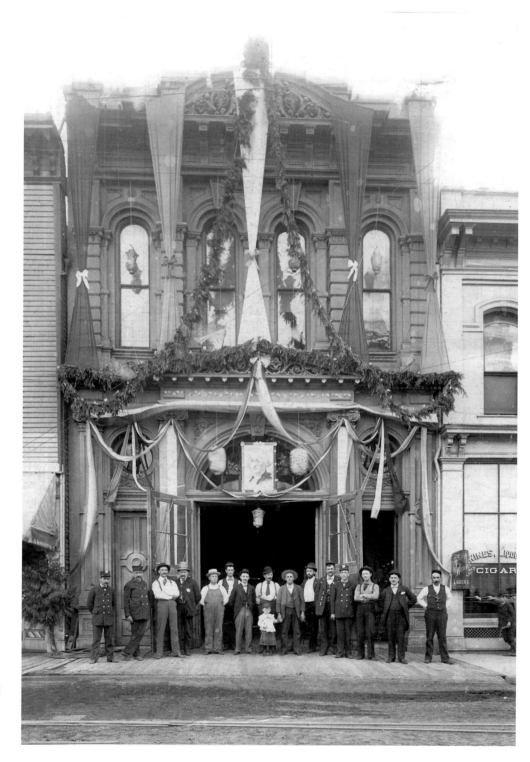

Fourth of July decorations at the
Hose & Chemical 2 fire station
on Southwest First Street in 1896

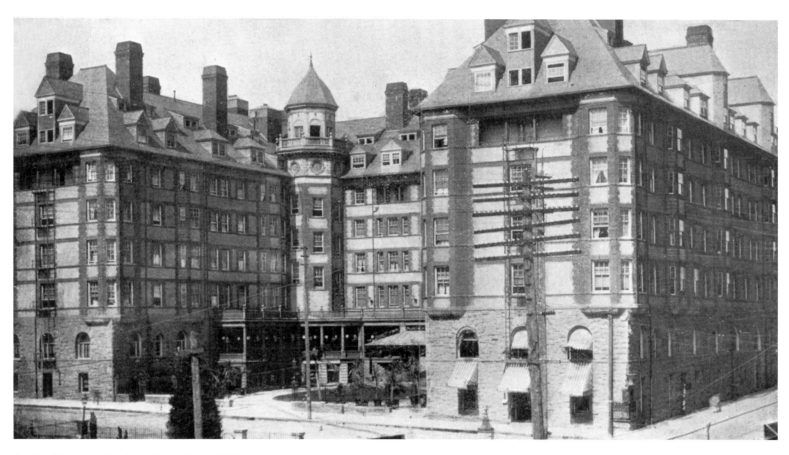

Portland Hotel at Sixth and Morrison, 1897

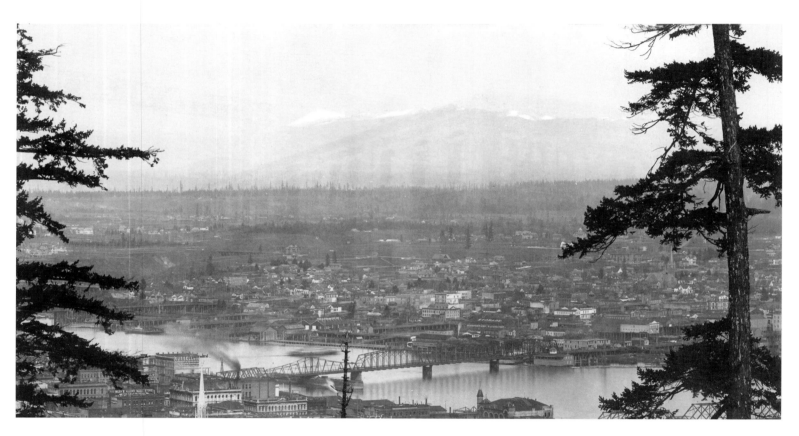

Eastside waterfront, circa 1897. Many streets were built on trestles. Structures were built on pilings.

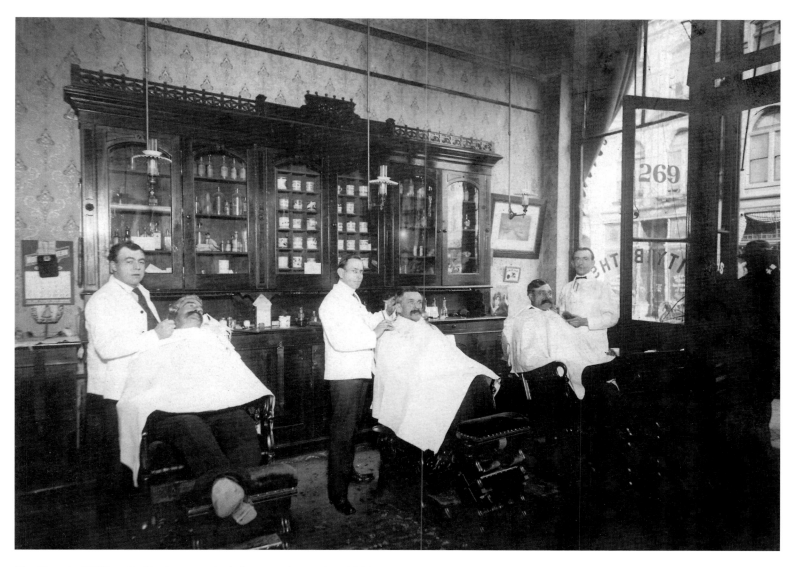

Fire Captain William R. Kerrigan, on the left, gets a shave, circa 1898.

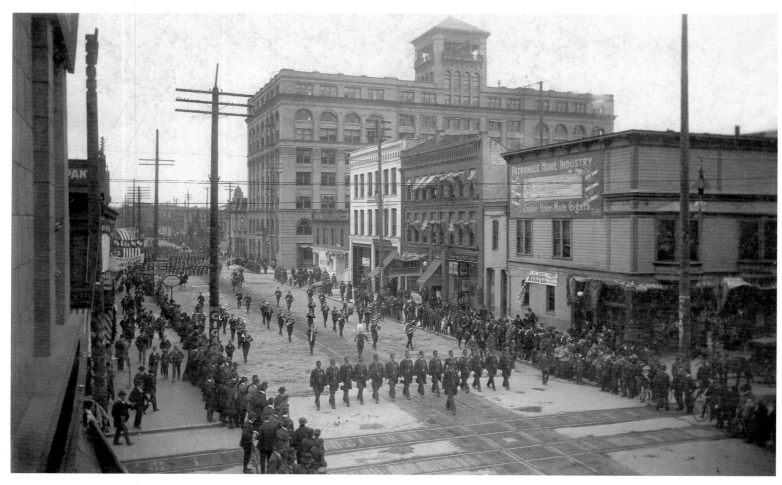

Spanish American War Parade on Fourth Street led by Portland Policemen in 1898.

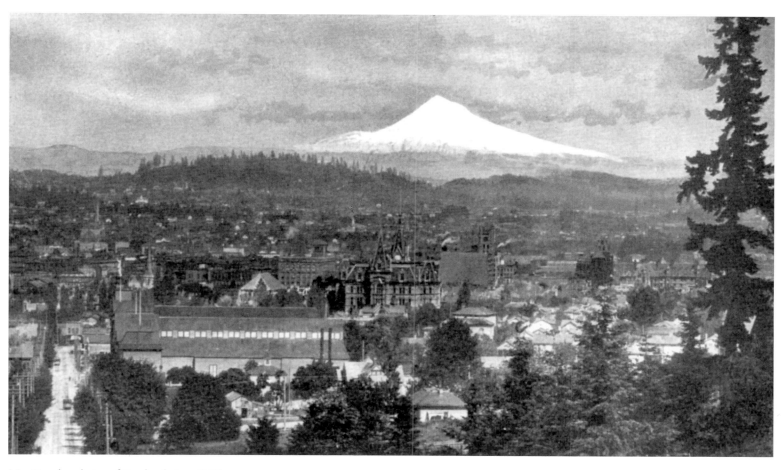

Mt. Hood and city of Portland circa 1899

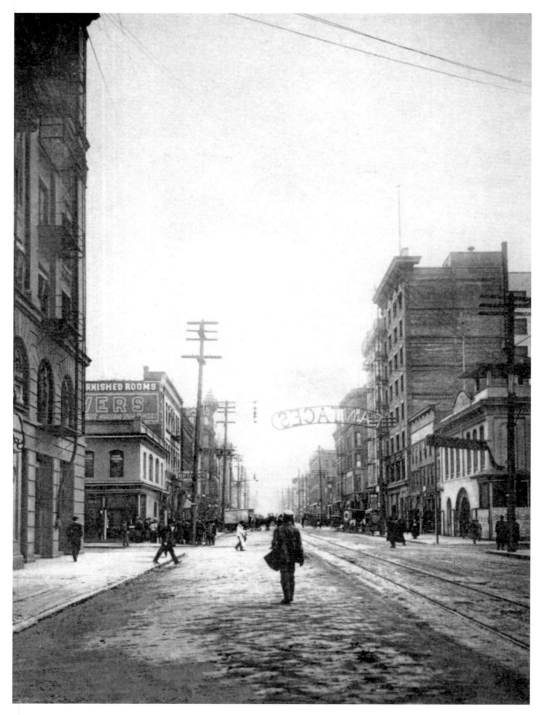

A 1907 view of Fourth Street from Stark Street

THE CITY AT THE TURN OF THE CENTURY

1900–1919

As the new century began, city officials started making plans for the future. In 1903, the Portland Park board hired Olmsted Brothers Landscape Architects to create a parks plan, and President Theodore Roosevelt dedicated the base of Lewis and Clark Memorial at City Park. Streetcar extensions expanded into new housing developments.

The city became a rail transportation hub and had a busy port as well. Lumber-related industries continued to grow in importance.

In 1902, the Library Association of Portland subscription library was opened free to the general public. The Portland Art Museum moved into its own building in 1905.

Portland was in a growth pattern when the Lewis and Clark Centennial Exposition and American Pacific and Oriental Fair took place in 1905. Dramatic population increases in the city occurred in the ensuing years. The downtown area was transformed as blocks of old frame buildings were removed for office buildings. Many elegant residences were transformed into apartment buildings, boarding houses, and hospitals as prominent families moved to the nearby suburbs.

Former farmlands begin yielding crops of homes as subdivisions took over agricultural property. Banker W. S. Ladd's Hazel Fern farm was transformed into the Laurelhurst development around 1910.

Prohibition started in the State of Oregon in 1916. Portland saloons closed or were transformed into soft drink parlors or restaurants. Weinhard's Brewery began producing soft drinks.

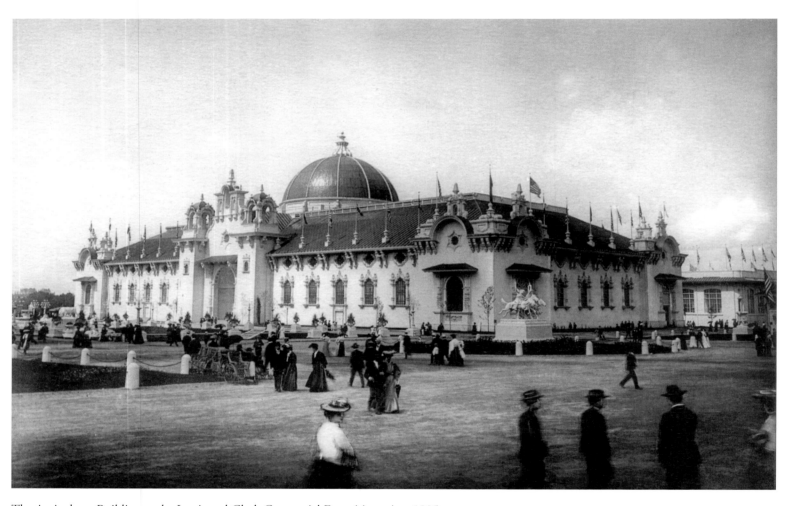

The Agriculture Building at the Lewis and Clark Centennial Exposition, circa 1905

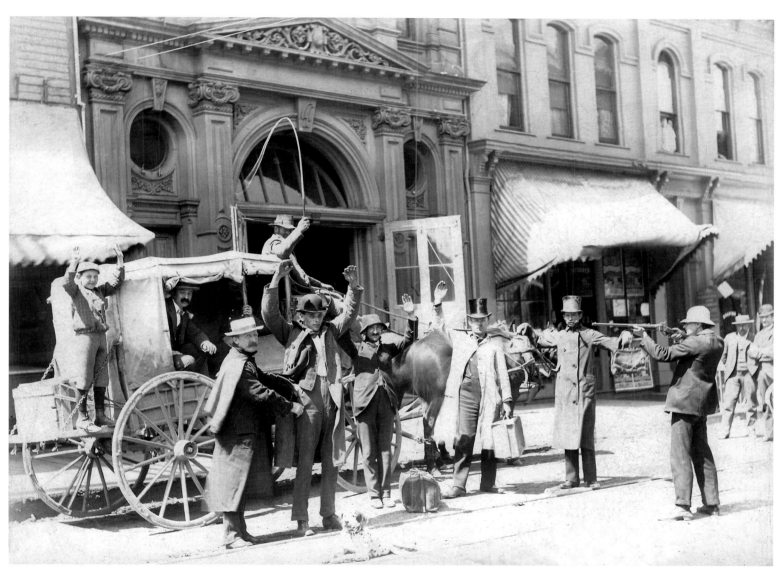

Theatrical troupe poses for an advertising photo in front of Hose 2 Fire Station on First Street, circa 1900.

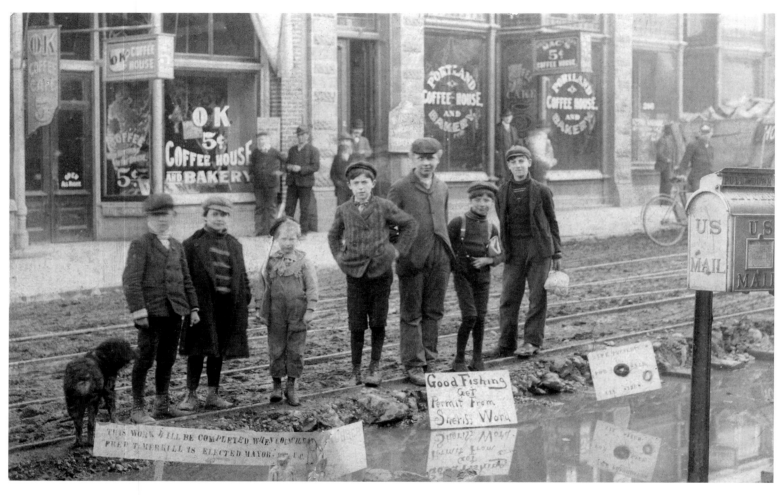

Children (near political signs) in front of the Portland and OK coffee houses, circa 1900

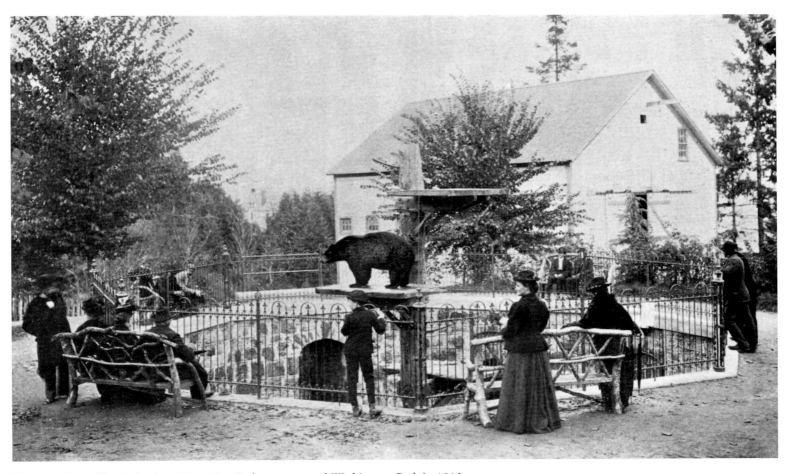

The Bear Pit at City Park, circa 1902. City Park was renamed Washington Park in 1912.

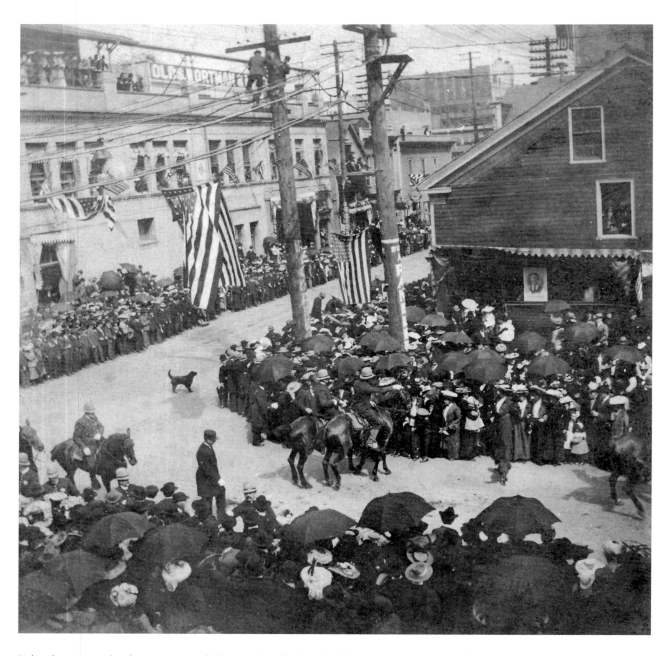

Police horse patrol policemen control the crowd at Sixth and Alder awaiting the parade for President Theodore Roosevelt, who after this event would dedicate the base of the Lewis and Clark Memorial at City Park, May 1903.

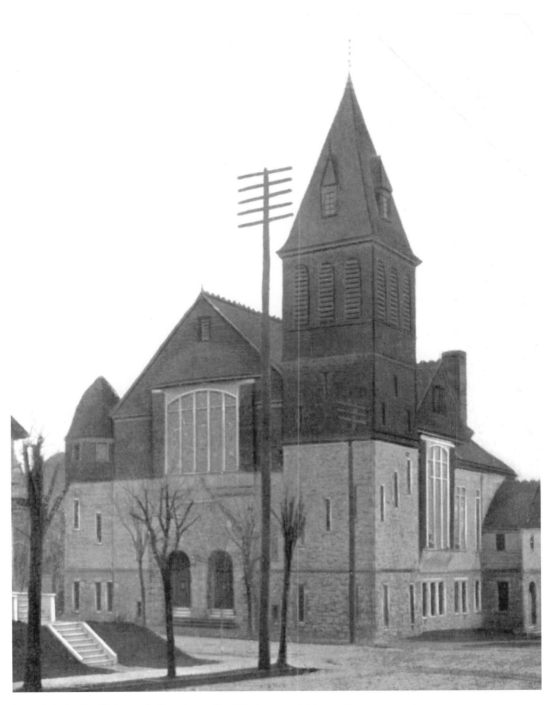

Grace Methodist Episcopal Church on Twelfth Street, which was later renamed
First Methodist Church, circa 1904.

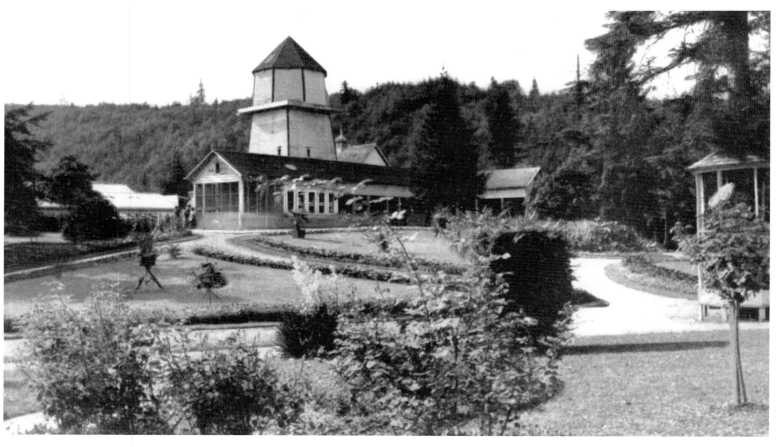

This view of City Park shows flower-rimmed paths leading to the animal houses of the zoo, circa 1904.

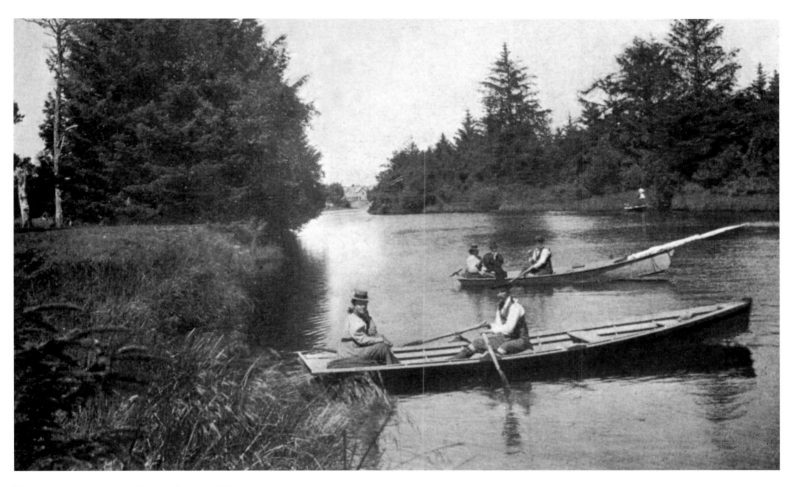

Boating on a stream in Portland, circa 1904

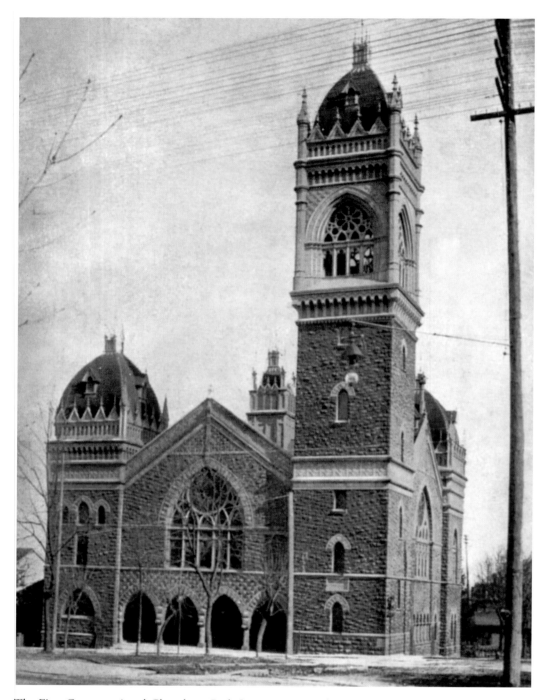

The First Congregational Church on Park Street, circa 1904

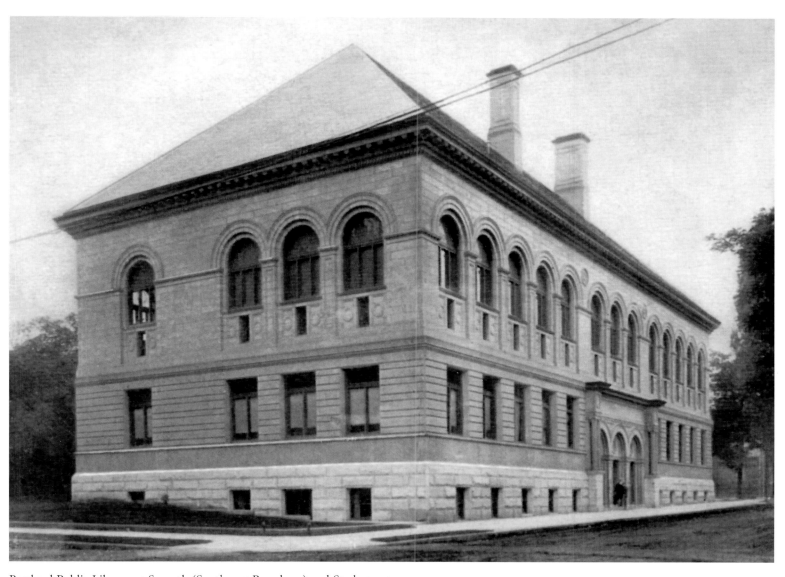

Portland Public Library, at Seventh (Southwest Broadway) and Stark streets

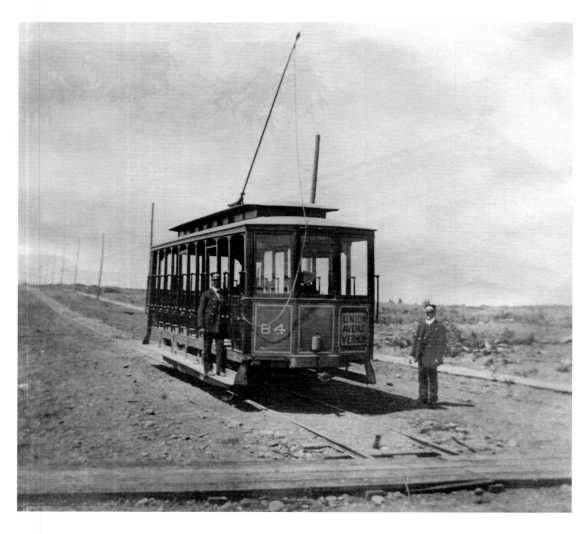

The Union Avenue–Vernon Streetcar at the end of the line, circa 1904

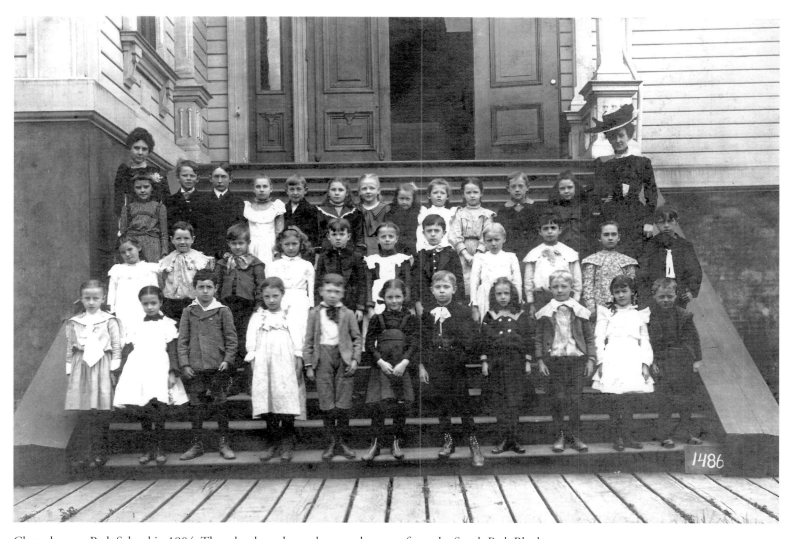

Class photo at Park School in 1904. The school was located across the street from the South Park Blocks.

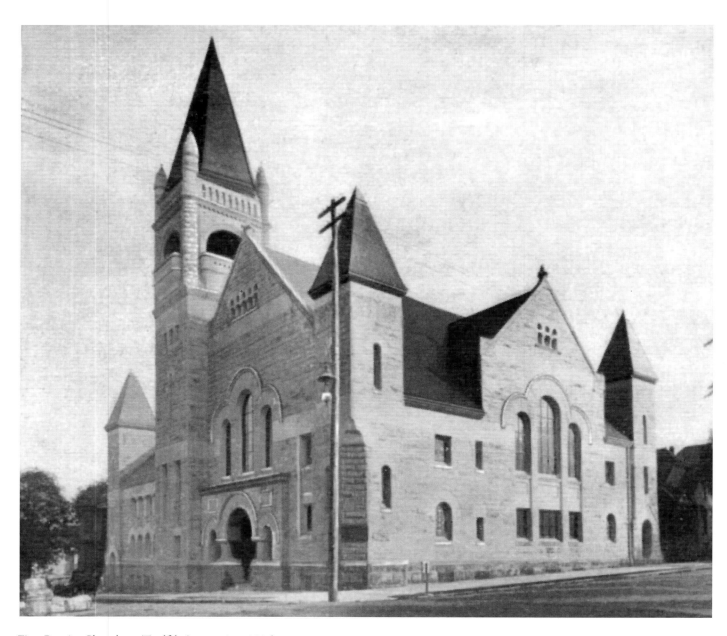

First Baptist Church on Twelfth Street, circa 1904

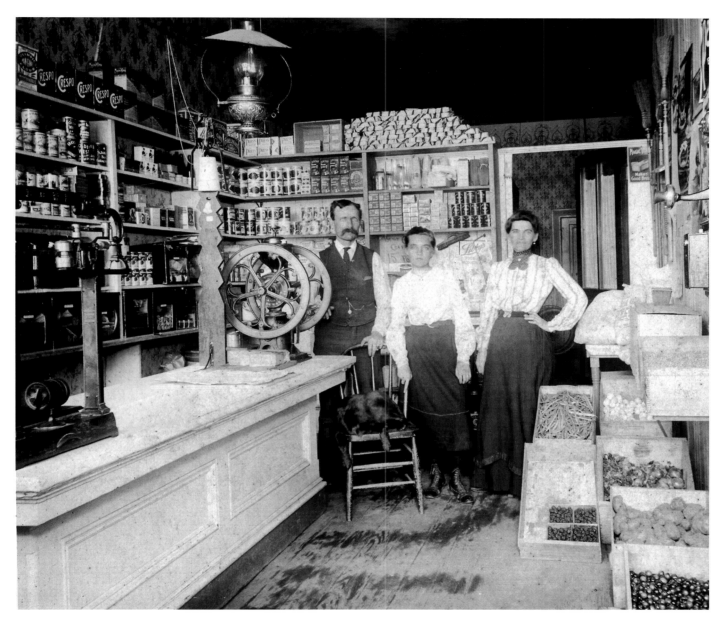

R. C. Walworth and family grocery store on North Russell Street, circa 1905

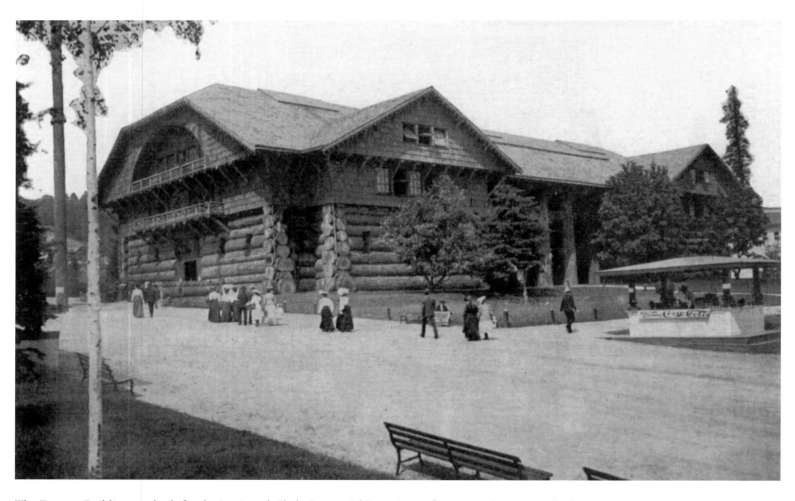

The Forestry Building was built for the Lewis and Clark Centennial Exposition of 1905. Within it were displays of forest products and photos of Native Americans by Edward S. Curtis, circa 1905.

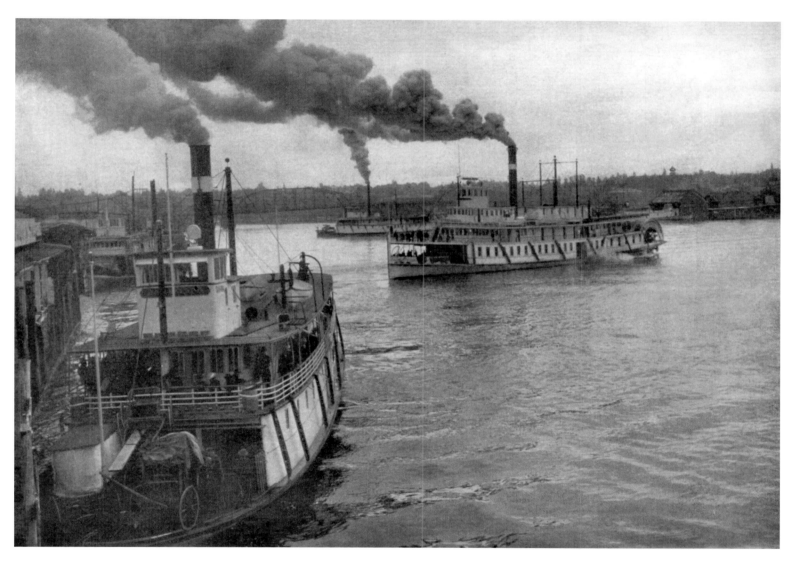

Steamboats on the Willamette River, circa 1905

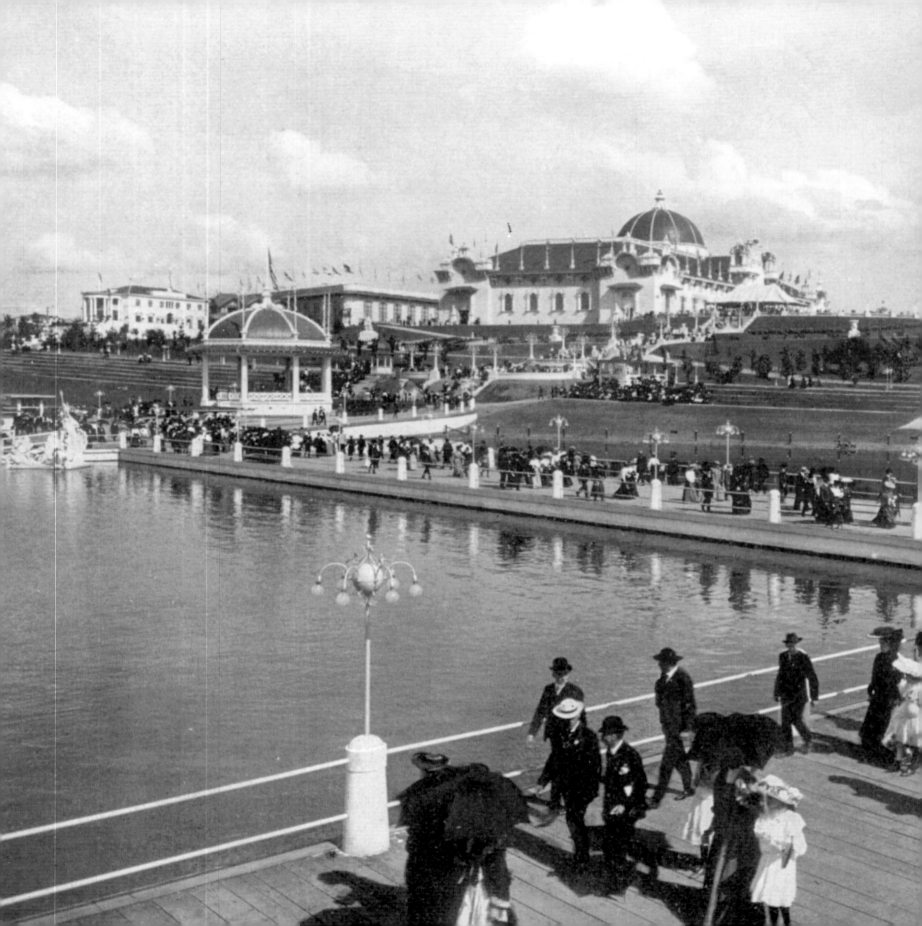

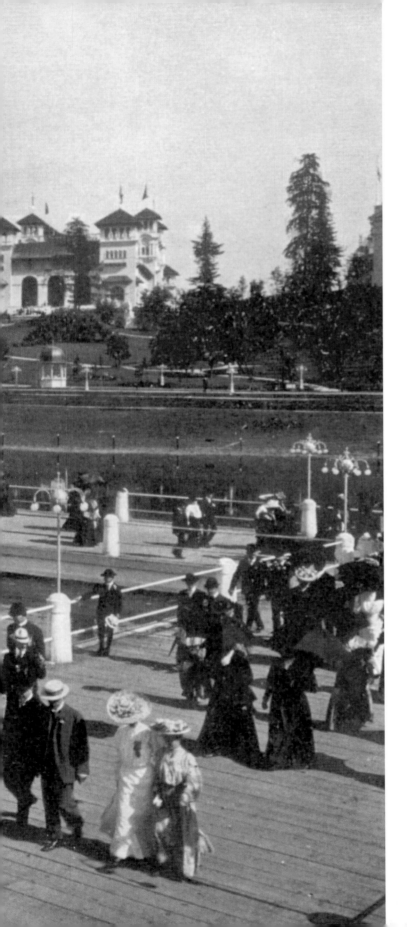

Part of the grounds of the Lewis and Clark Centennial and American Pacific Exposition and Oriental Fair of 1905

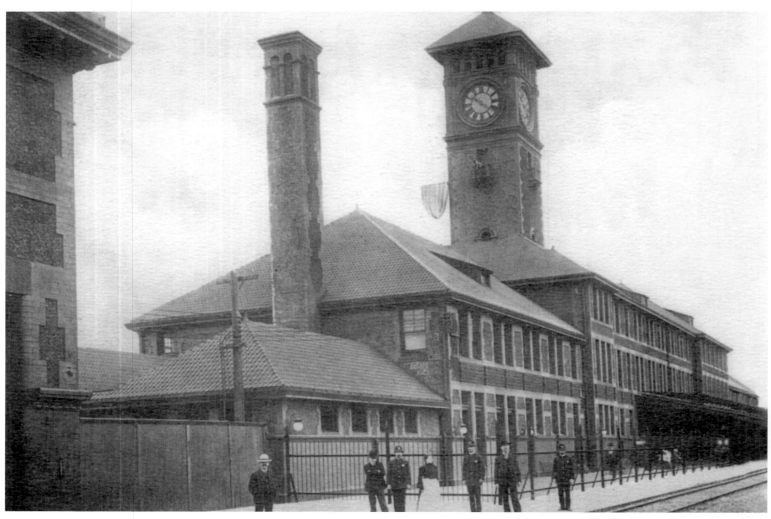

Union Station in 1905

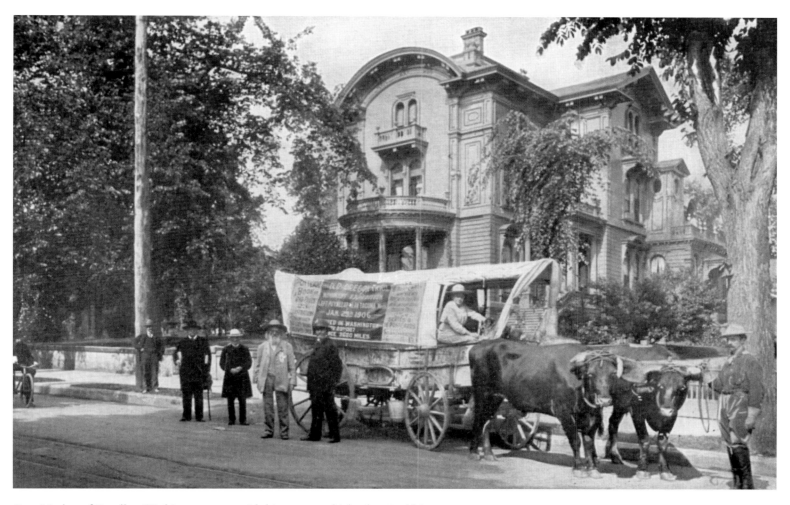

Ezra Meeker of Puyallup Washington poses with his wagon, which advertised his "Old Oregon Trail Monument Expedition" of 1906–1907. Meeker first crossed the Oregon Trail in 1852. Photo circa 1907

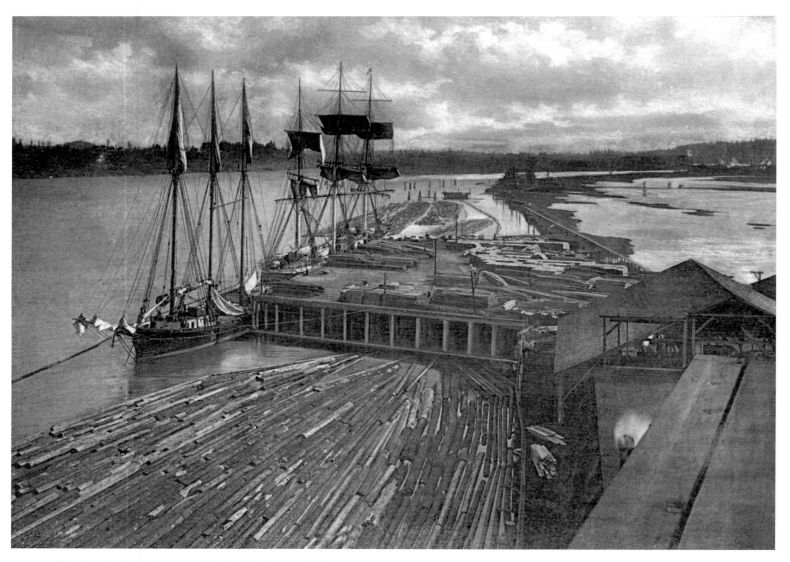

A sawmill loading dock on the upper Portland harbor in 1907

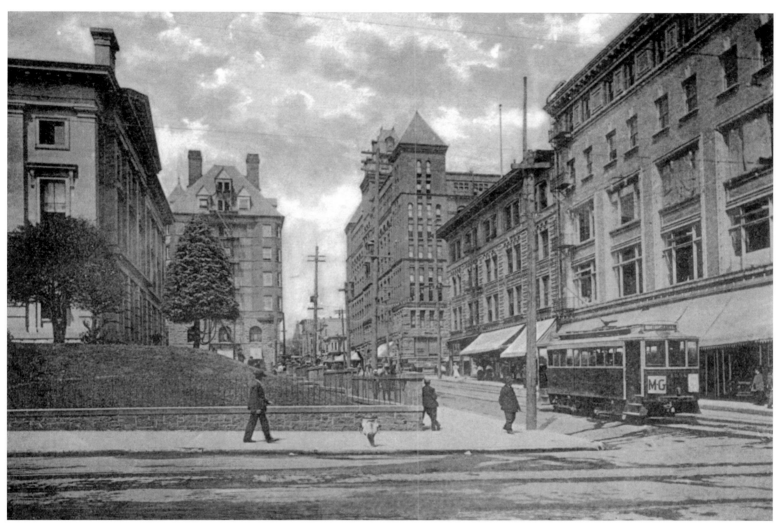

Looking west on Morrison Street from Fifth Street. Buildings, from left to right, are the
Post Office, Hotel Portland, and the Marquam Building. The Meier & Frank
Department Store is to the right of the streetcar, circa 1907.

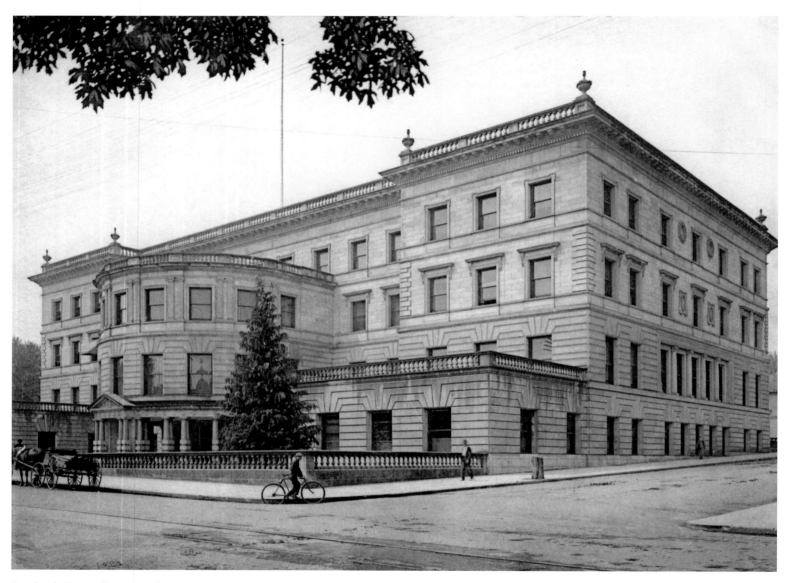

Portland City Hall on Fourth Street, circa 1907. At this time the City Museum, which was a natural history museum, and the Oregon Historical Society, occupied a portion of this building.

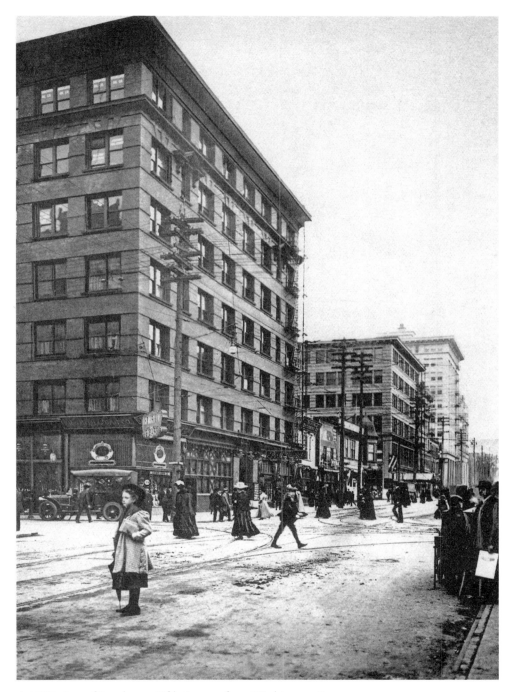

A 1907 view of Southwest Fifth Avenue from Washington Street

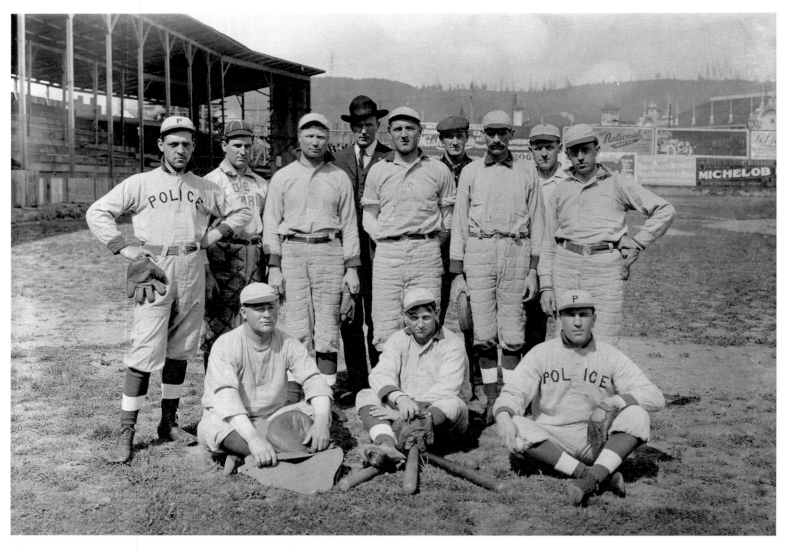

The Portland Police baseball team at Vaughn Street Ballpark, circa 1908. Buildings from the 1905 Lewis and Clark Centennial Exposition are in the background.

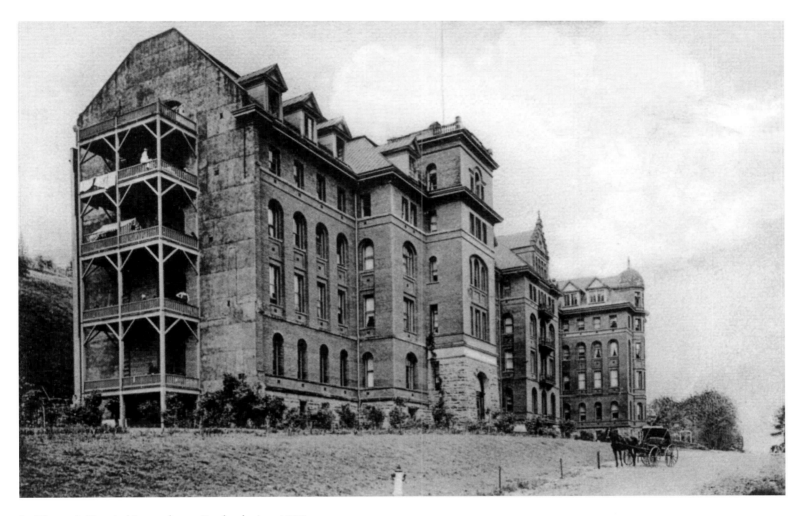

St. Vincent's Hospital in northwest Portland, circa 1909

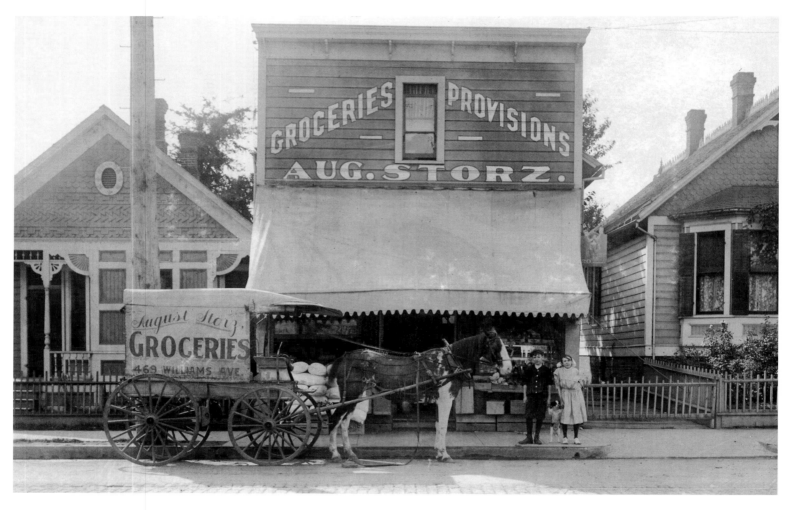

August Storz grocery and provisions store on North Williams Avenue in 1910

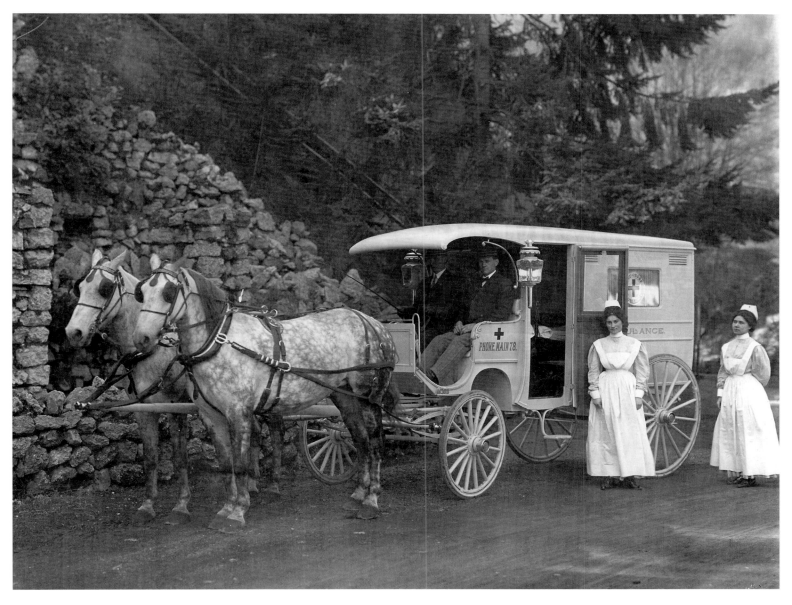

The Red Cross Ambulance Company's horse-drawn ambulance with nurses at the entrance to City Park in 1910

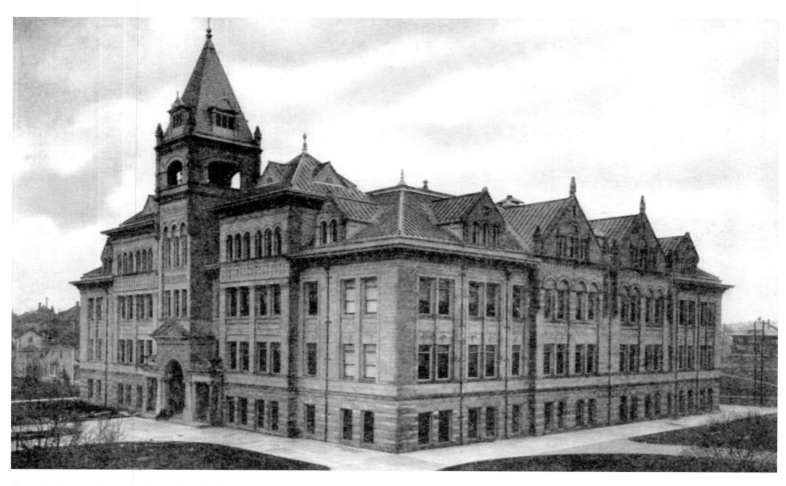

Opening in 1906, East Side High School was renamed Washington High School in 1909. This photo is circa 1910.

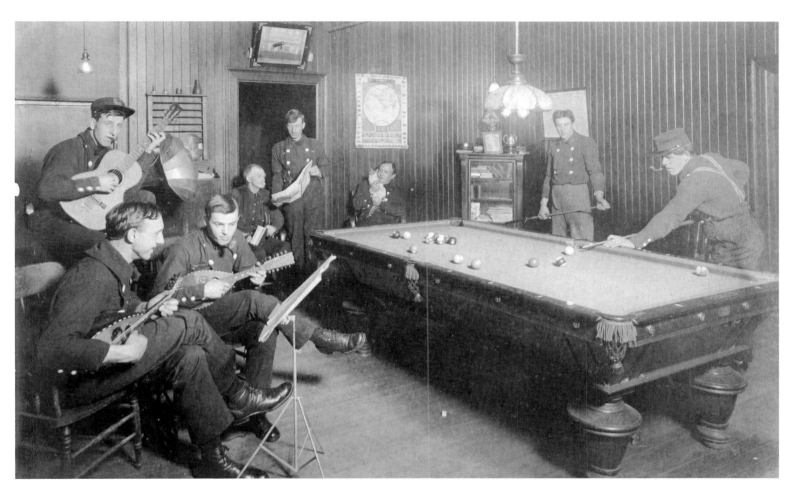

Firemen's living quarters at Station 15, circa 1910

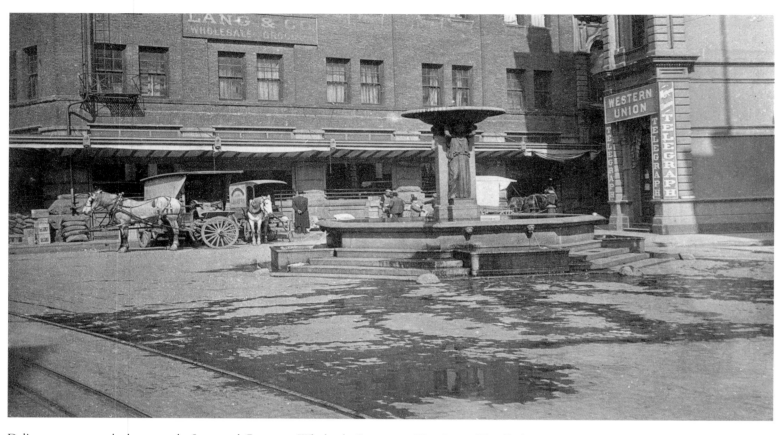

Delivery wagons parked next to the Lang and Company Wholesale Grocery on First Street. The Skidmore Fountain and an office for the Western Union Telegraph Company are on the right, circa 1910s.

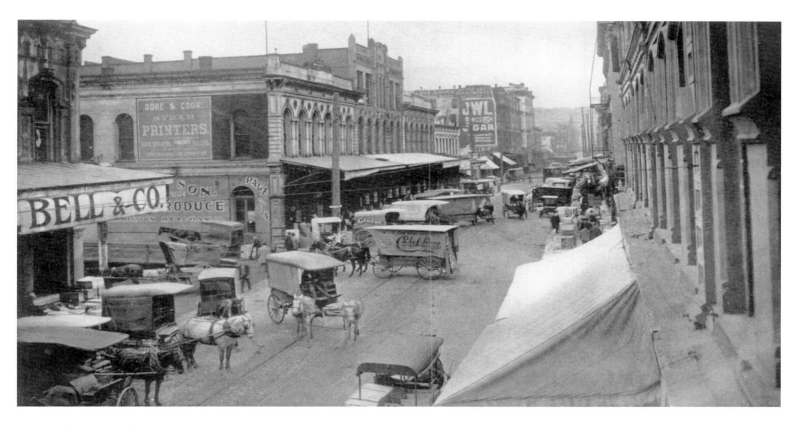

A view of wagons and businesses along Front Avenue, circa 1910

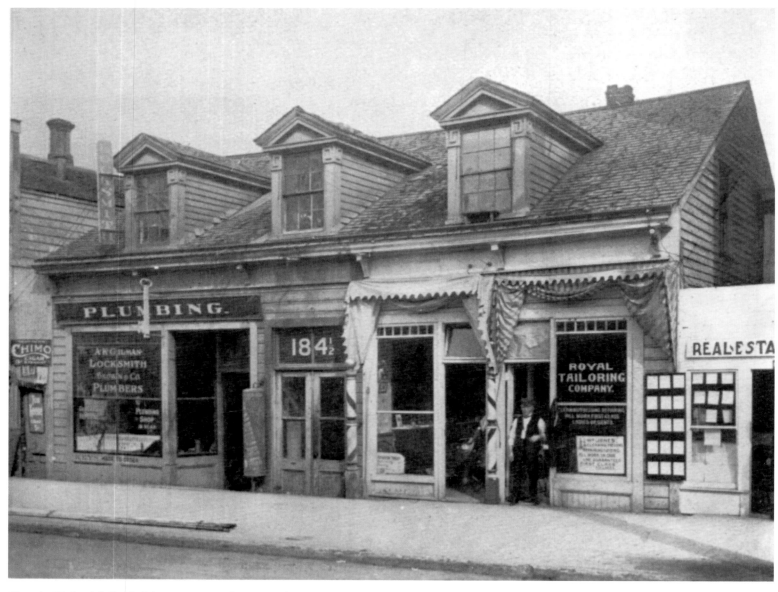

Captain Nathaniel Crosby's home on Fourth Street. This was Portland's first frame house, built in 1847, which was moved from its original location on First Street in 1860. In 1910, it contained barber, plumbing, and tailor shops.

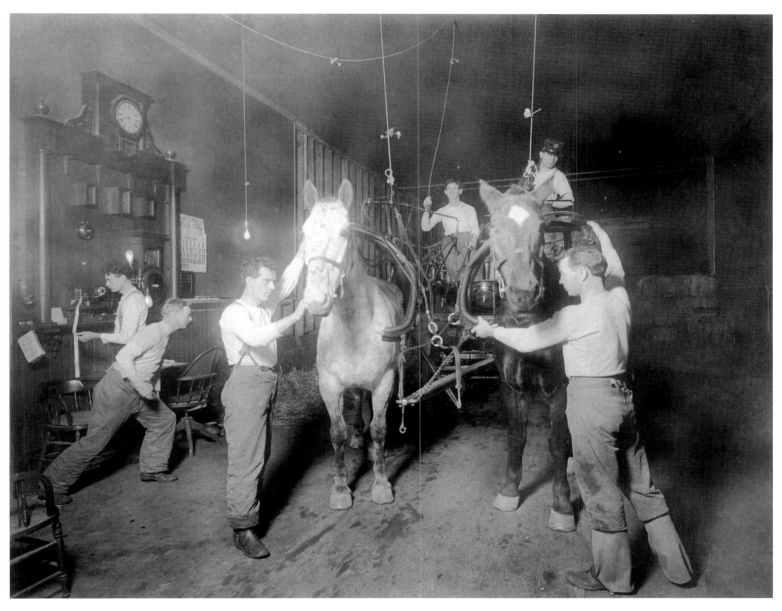

Fire horses being harnessed to a fire engine, circa 1910

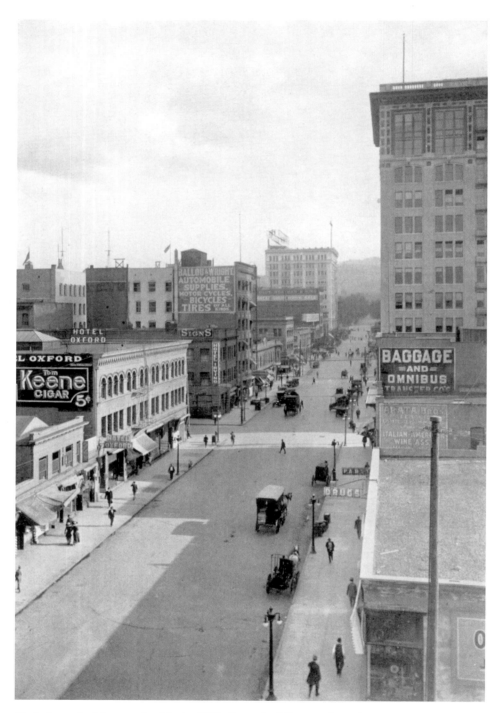

Sixth Street looking south with the Wells Fargo Building on the right, circa 1910

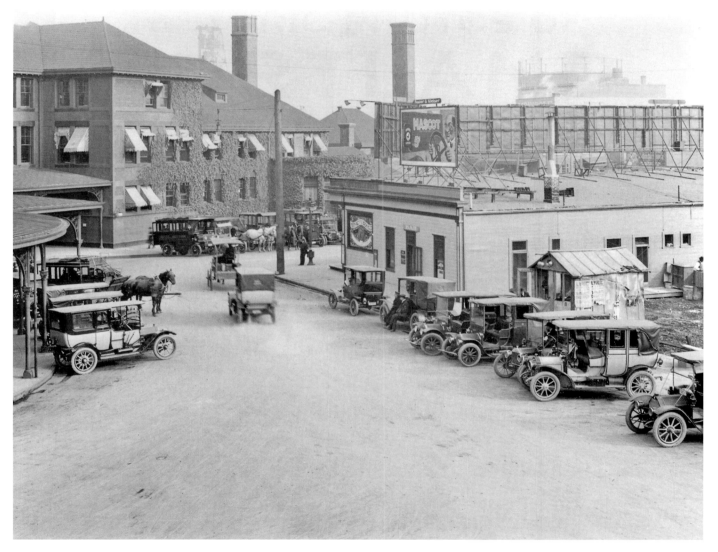

At Union Station, assorted vehicles await passengers for pickup and delivery to area hotels, circa 1910.

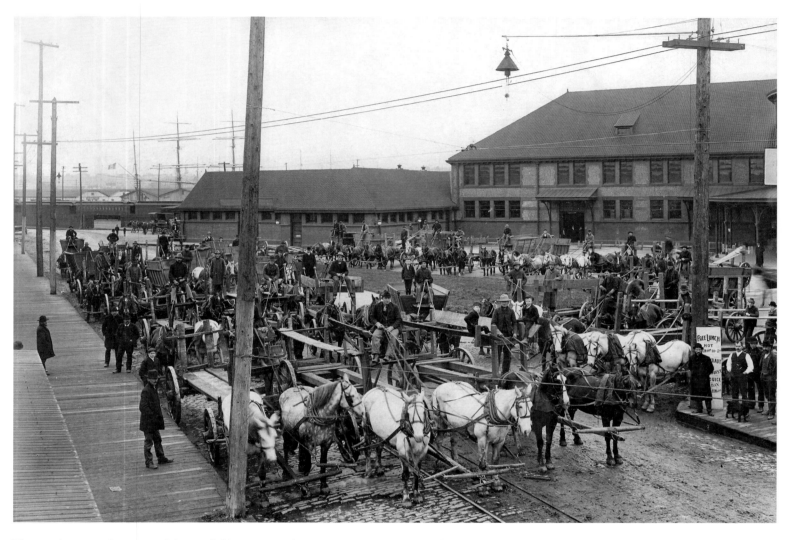

The employees and wagons of the Banfield Veysey Fuel Company pose next to Portland's Union Station, circa 1910.

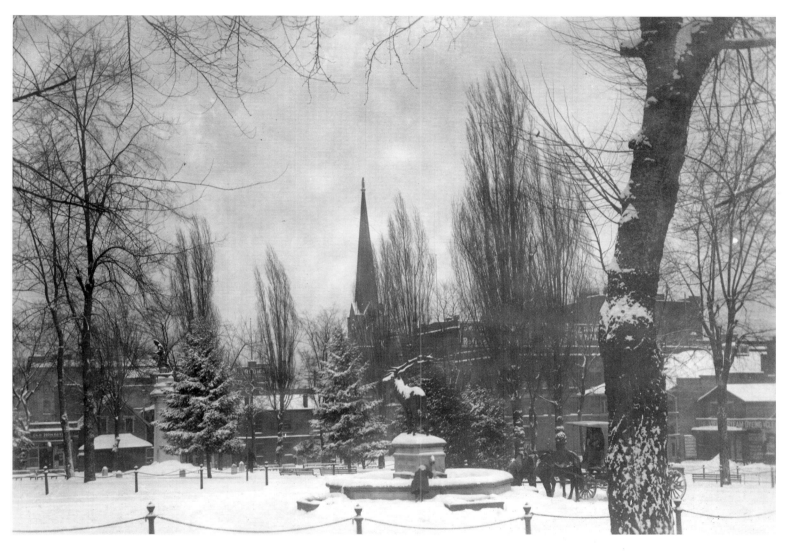

Lownsdale Square of the Plaza Blocks, circa 1910. At the center is the Thompson Elk Fountain, which was given to the city by former Mayor D. P. Thompson.

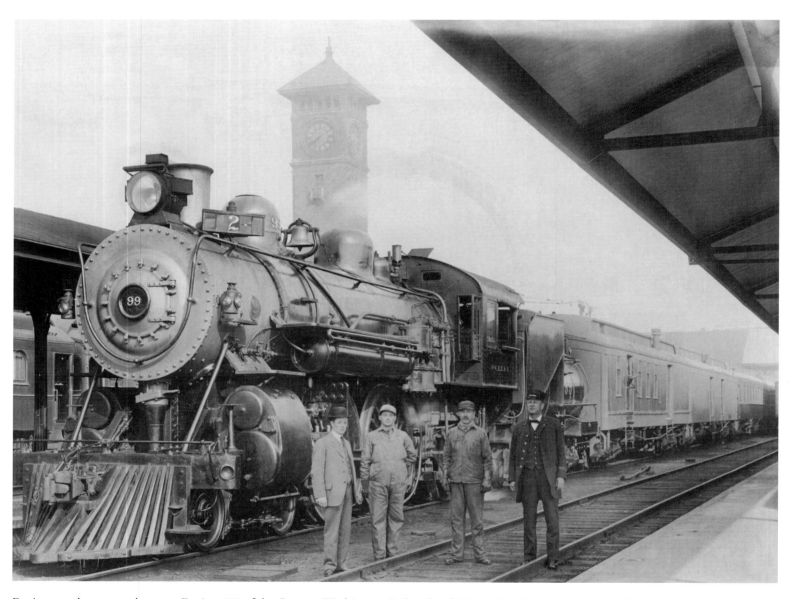

Engineer and crew stand next to Engine #99 of the Oregon, Washington Railroad and Navigation Company at Union Station, circa 1910.

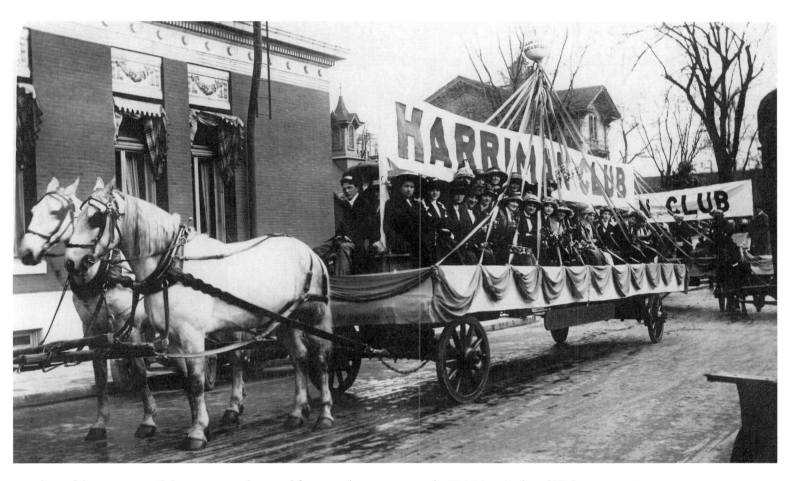

Members of the Harriman Club on a wagon decorated for a parade, pose next to the YMCA at Sixth and Taylor streets, circa 1910.

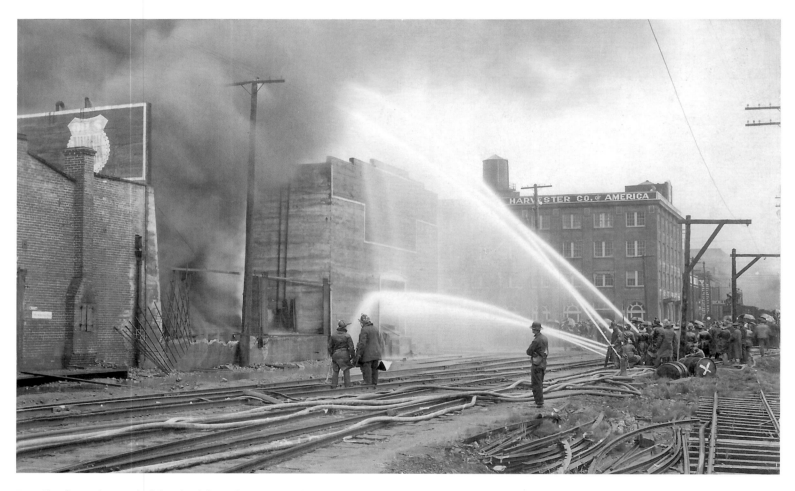

Fire Chief David Campbell lost his life in the Union Oil Fire on June 26, 1911. Fearing that firemen were still in the building, he entered to save them. The building exploded and collapsed with him inside.

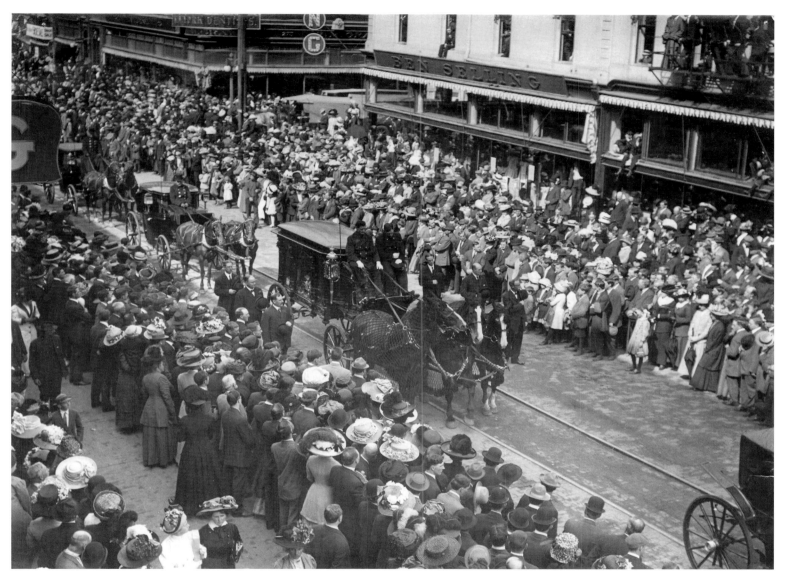

Chief David Campbell's funeral on June 28, 1911. Honored and respected by many, he was referred to as "Our Dave," and people lined the street to observe his funeral procession. The hearse was pulled by his three favorite horses.

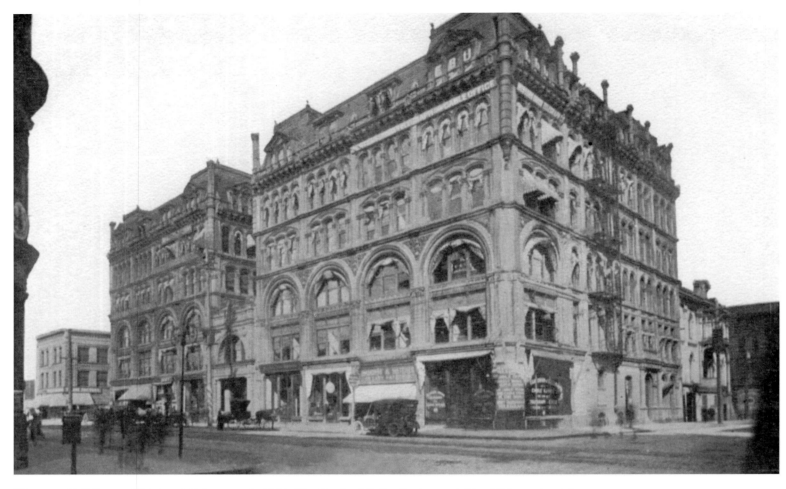

Worcester Building on Third and Oak streets in 1911. The Portland Police Station and City Jail is on the right.

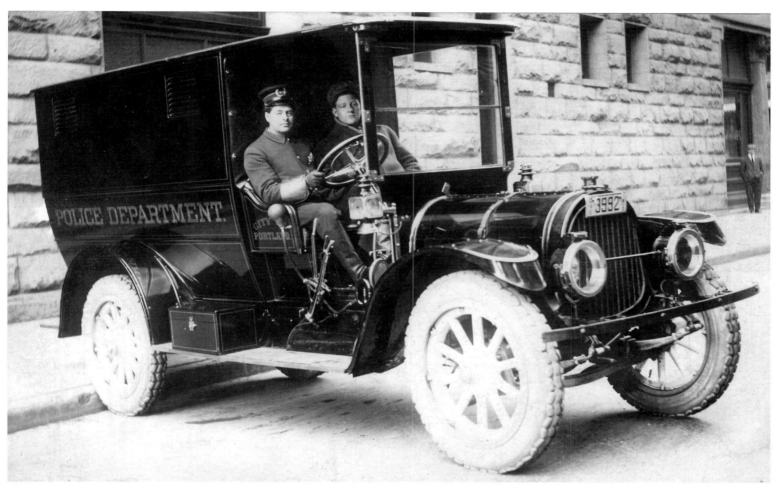

The Police Department's Pope Hartford patrol wagon parked beside the Portland Trust Bank in 1912

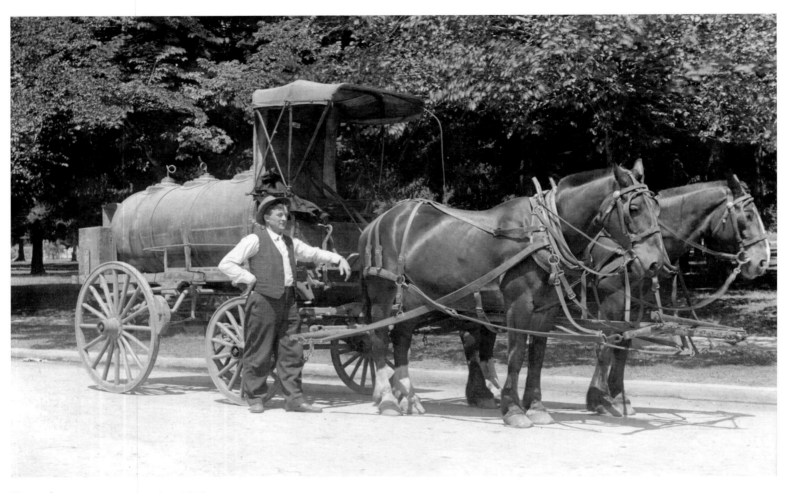

Horse-drawn water wagon, circa 1912

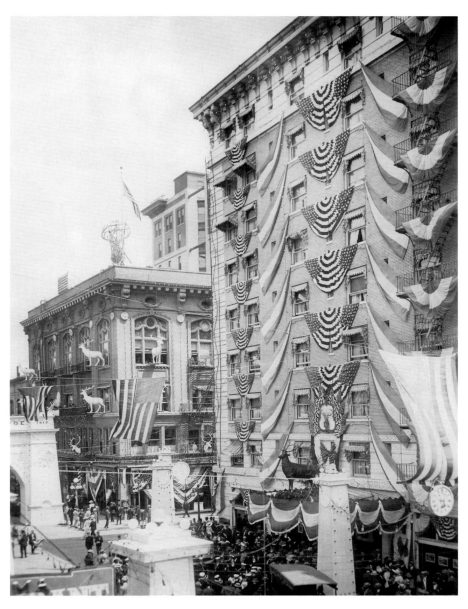

View of the Elk's Building at Seventh (Southwest Broadway) and Stark
during the Elk's 1912 Convention. On the right is the Imperial Hotel.

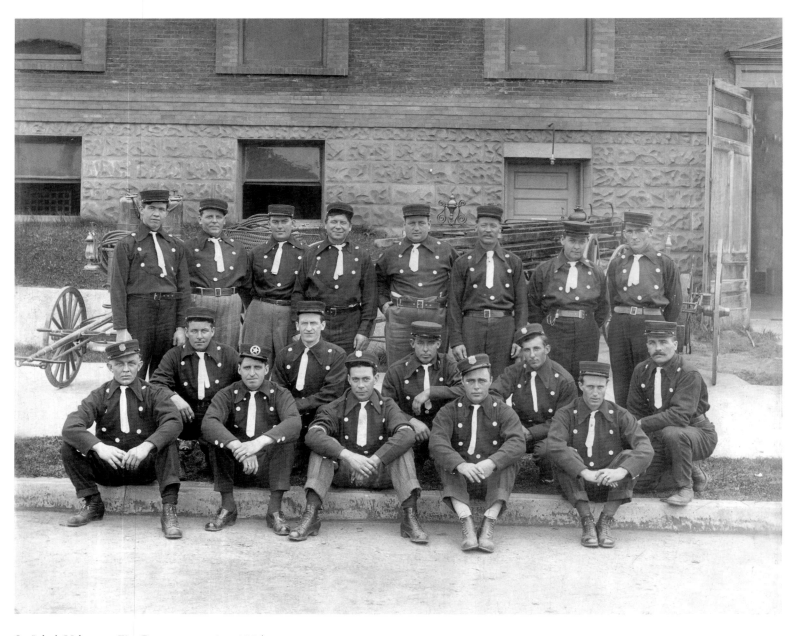

St. John's Volunteer Fire Department, circa 1914

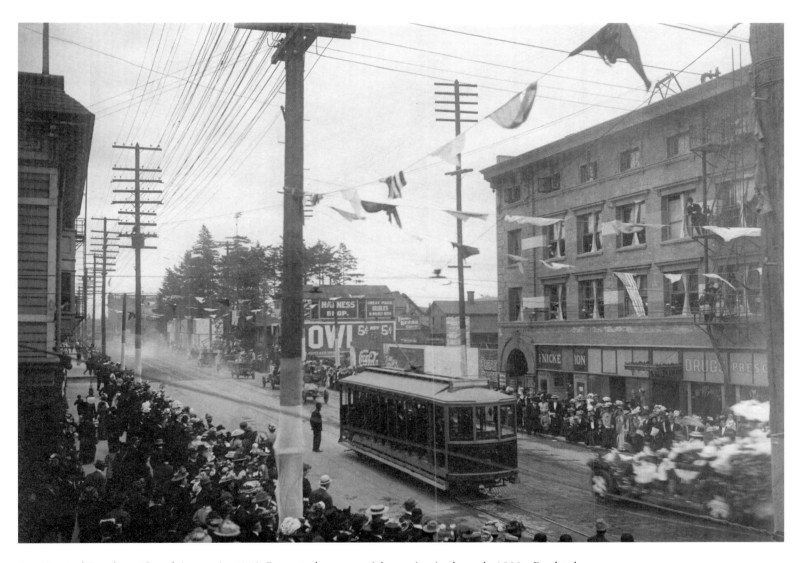

Rose Festival Parade on Grand Avenue in 1915. Roses took on a special meaning in the early 1900s. Portland became known as the Rose City.

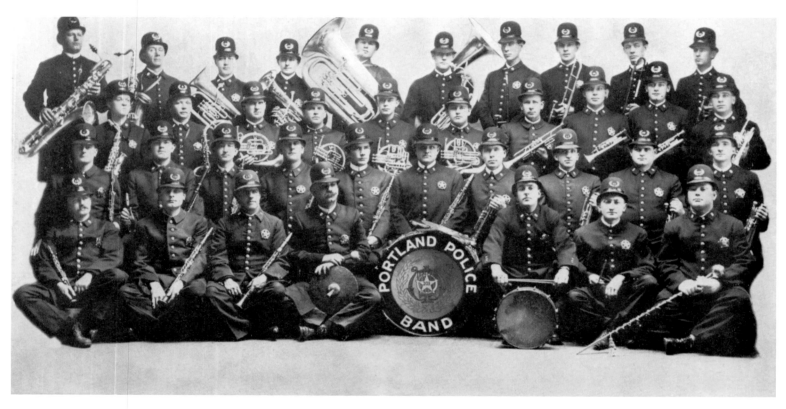

Portland Police Band in 1915

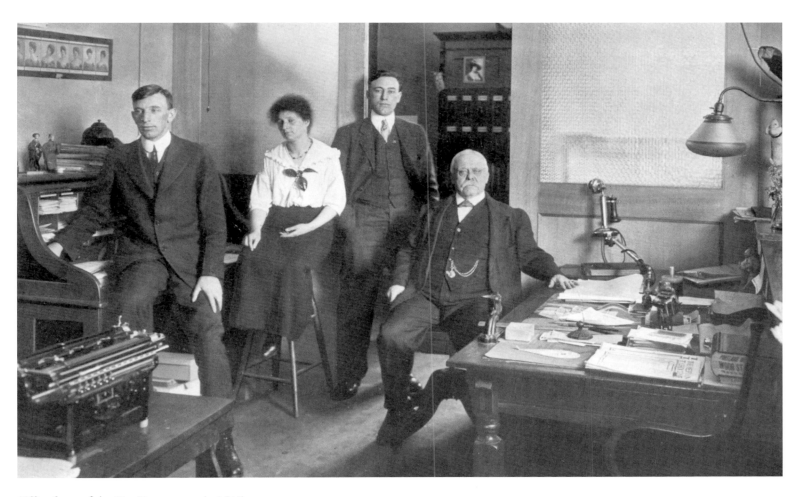

Office force of the Fire Department in 1915

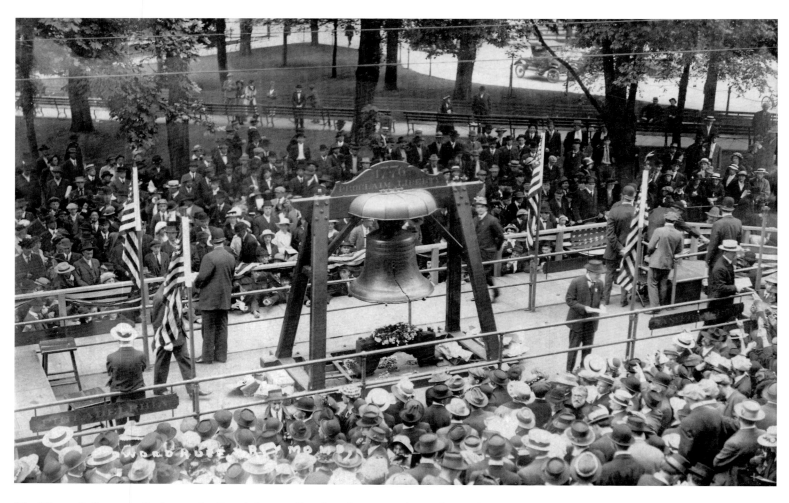

The Liberty Bell was on display on the Fourth Street railroad tracks next to the Multnomah County Courthouse in July 1915. The Liberty Bell was en route to the Panama Pacific Exposition in San Francisco. (In the background is Lownsdale Square of the Plaza Blocks.)

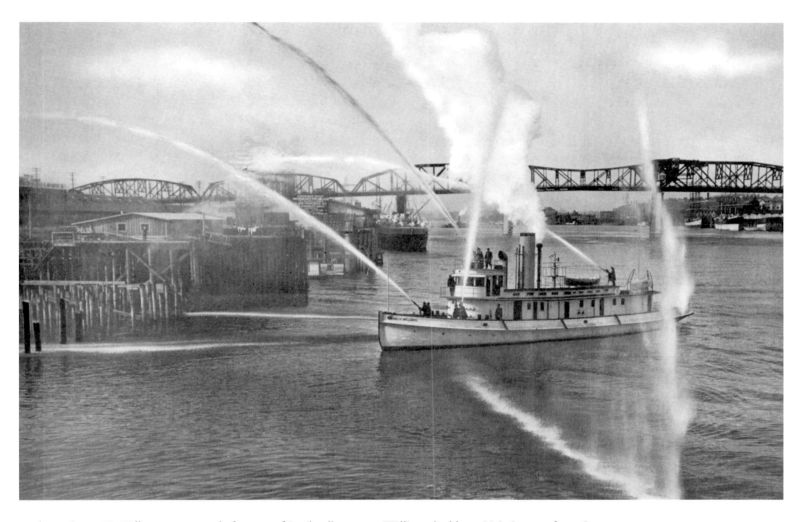

Fireboat *George H. Williams* was named after one of Portland's mayors. Williams had been U.S. Senator from Oregon in the 1860s and 1870s, later serving as Attorney General during President U. S. Grant's administration.

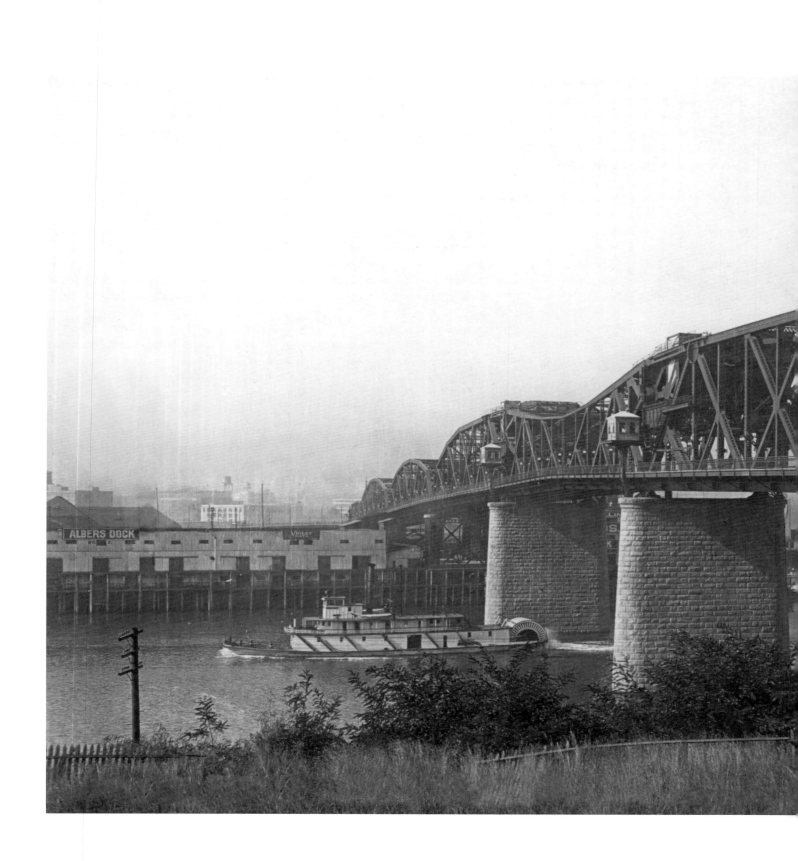

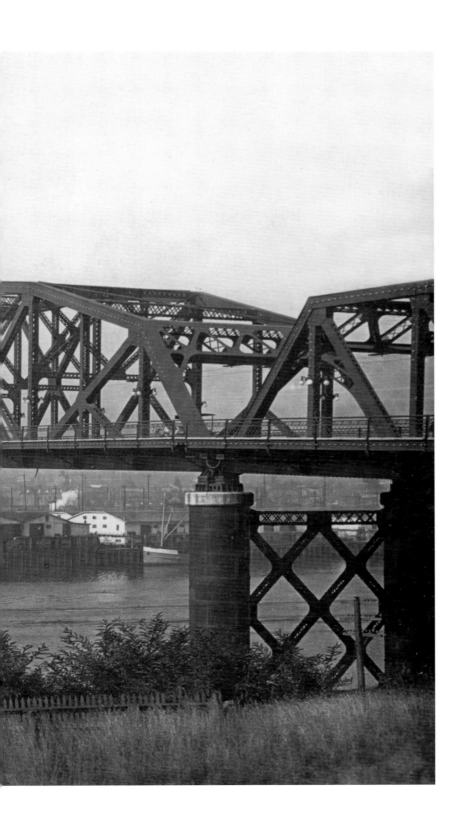

Broadway Bridge in 1915

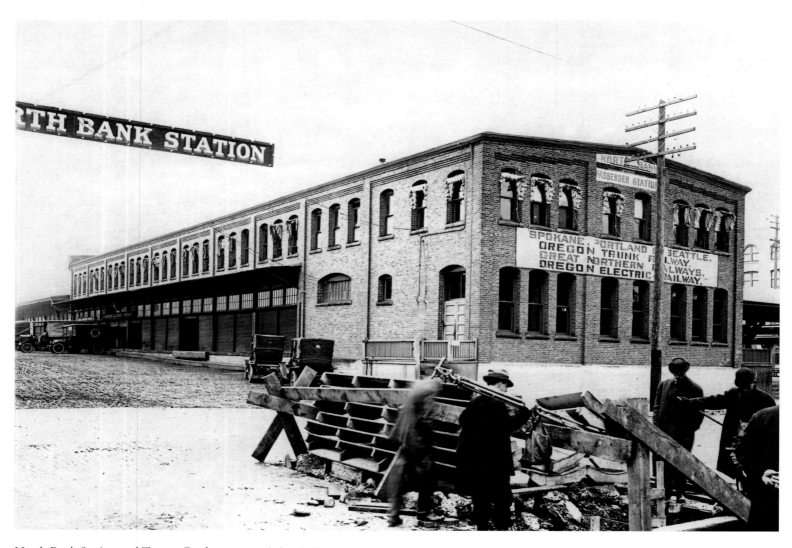

North Bank Station and Tanner Creek sewer repair in 1917

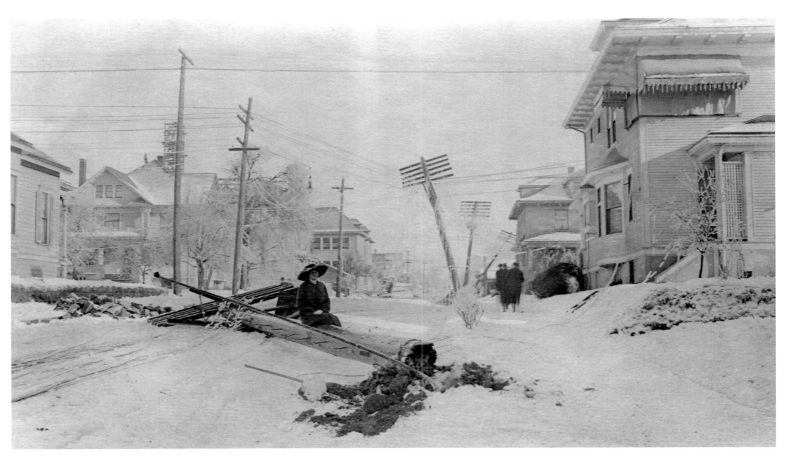

Northeast Weidler Street during ice storm in 1917

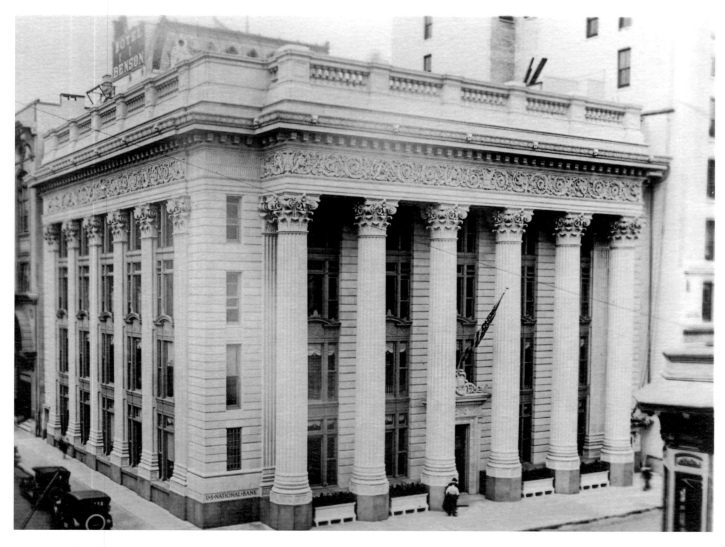

US National Bank on Sixth Street, circa 1918

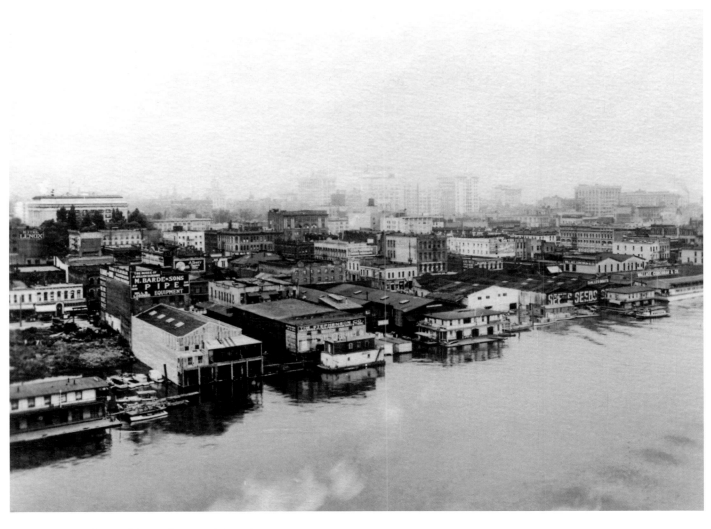

West side waterfront of the Willamette River, circa 1918

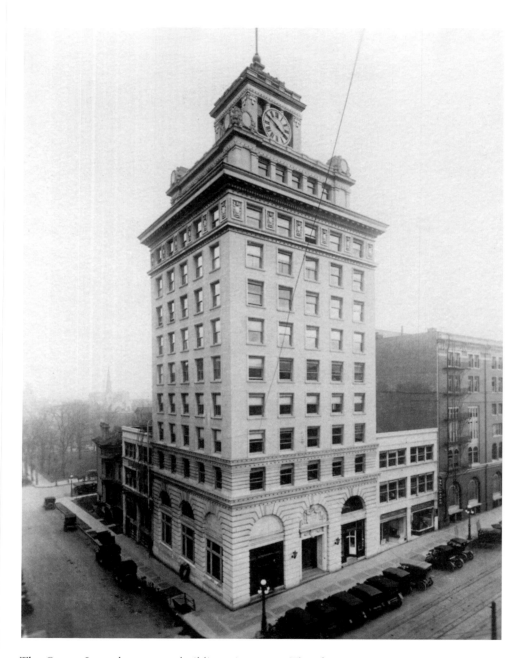

The *Oregon Journal* newspaper building, circa 1918. The afternoon
newspaper occupied this building from 1912 until moving into the old
Public Market Building on Front Avenue in 1948.

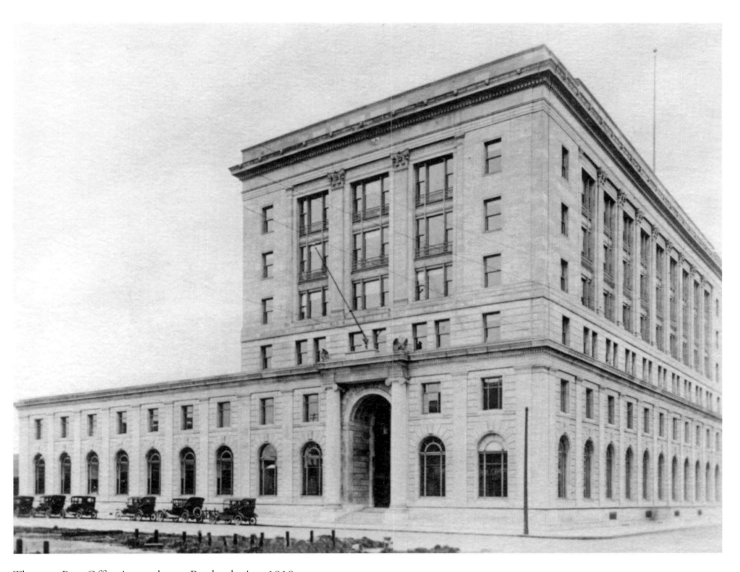

The new Post Office in northwest Portland, circa 1918

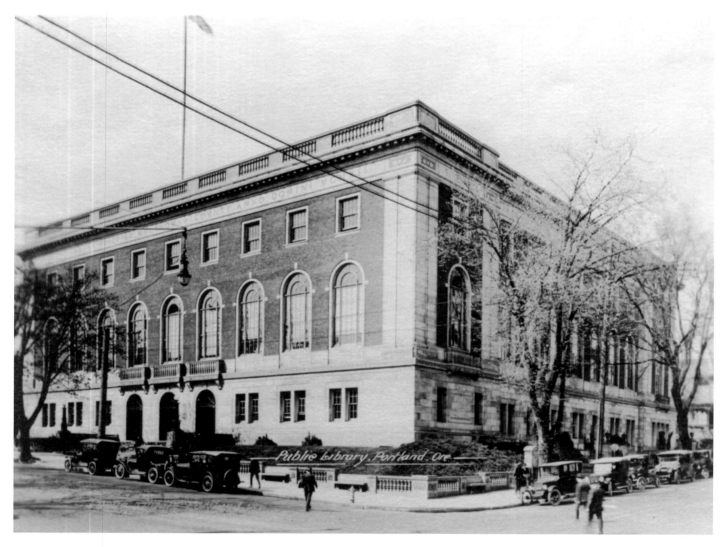

The Library Association of Portland vacated its old overcrowded building and moved into the new Central Library at Tenth and Yamhill streets in 1913.

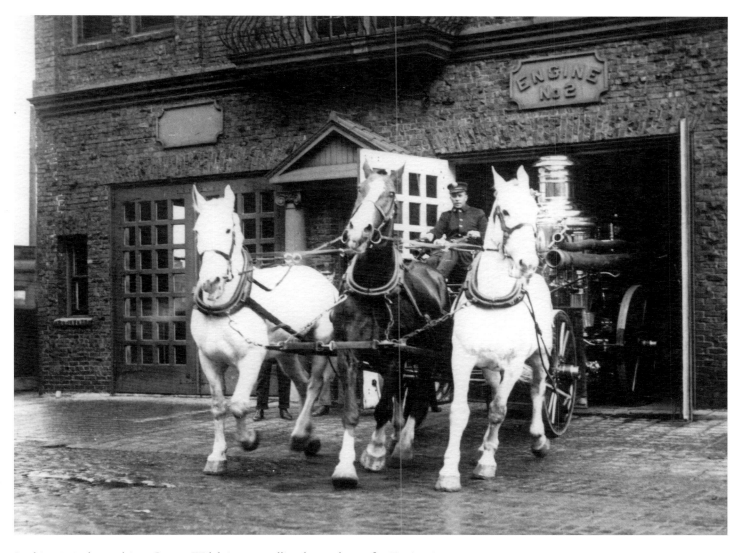

In this 1918 photo, driver George Welch is seen pulling horse-drawn fire Engine 2 out of the station.

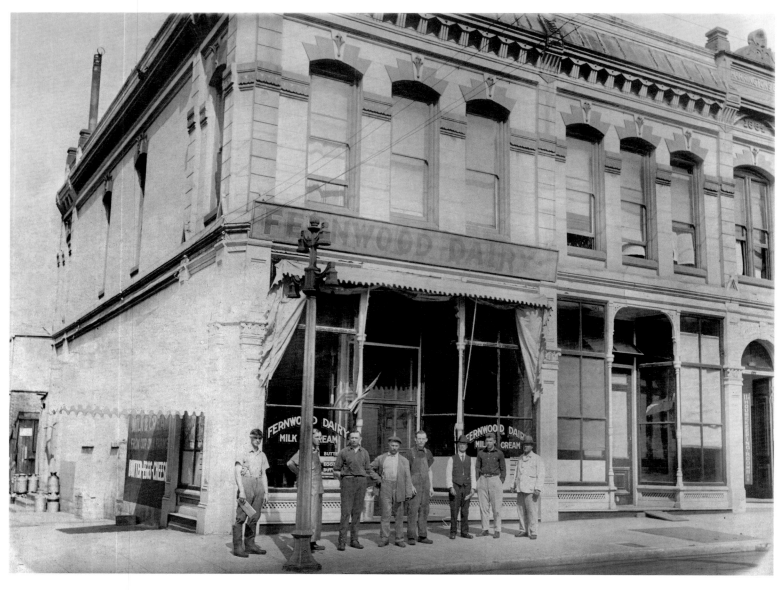

Fernwood Dairy, circa 1918 in Southeast Portland at 15 Union Avenue (later SE Martin Luther King Jr. Blvd.). The business was in Harrington's Block, which was erected in the mid 1880s.

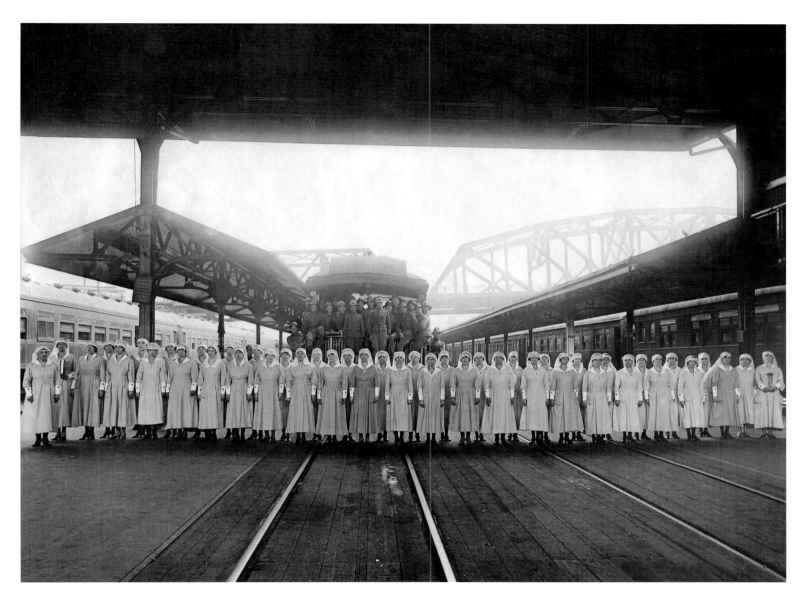

The American Red Cross Canteen volunteers outside Union Station on September 28, 1918. These women met the troop trains and distributed magazines, candy, cigarettes, and other items to soldiers.

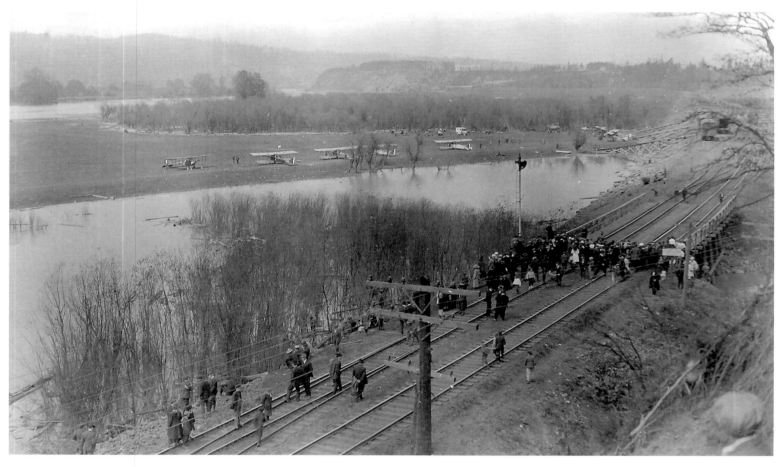

Airplanes at Mock's Bottom for 1919 war loan air show. Columbia University, today's University of Portland, can be seen in the distance.

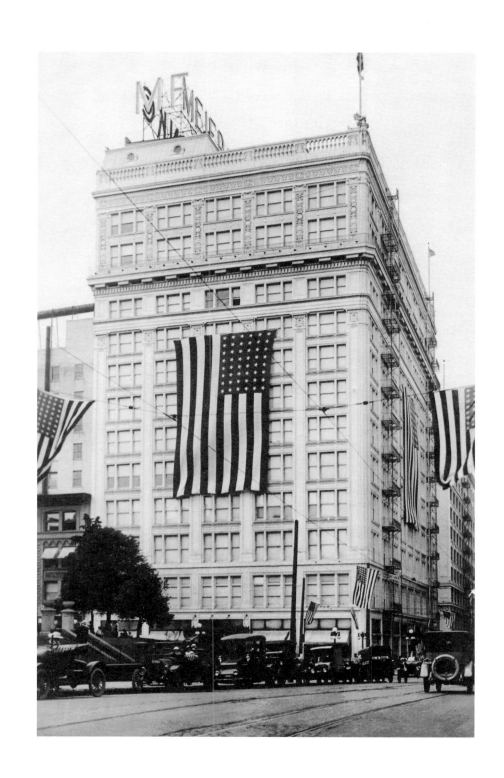

Meier and Frank Department Store
on Fifth and Morrison, circa 1919

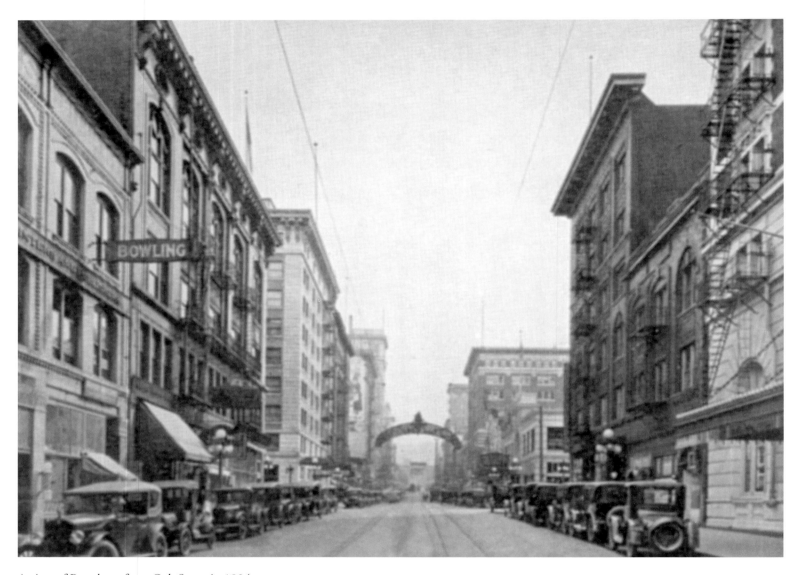

A view of Broadway from Oak Street in 1924

A Developing Metropolis

1920–1939

Escalating property values on downtown blocks caused many elegant residences to be sold for redevelopment. In the early 1920s the Failing residence was sold and was replaced by a multi-storied parking structure and the Public Service Building in 1926 and 1927. The J. N. Dolph residence also was torn down for parking. W. S. Ladd's residence came down and ended up as a parking lot, and a portion of the block was also used as a miniature golf course in 1930.

The Battleship *Oregon,* a historic relic of the Spanish American War, was lent to the State of Oregon in 1925 and became a floating maritime museum. The Port of Portland's Swan Island Airport opened in 1927. The old decaying docks at the waterfront were removed and replaced by a harbor wall in 1929.

The Depression brought the Works Progress Administration (WPA) government agency into city public works projects around 1935. A "Hooverville" of shacks was built by a community of out-of-work people near the railroad tracks in Sullivan's Gulch.

Emma Corbett, widow of Henry W. Corbett, died in 1936. After the furnishings of her house were sold at auction, the house was removed in 1937, replaced by the Central Bus Depot in 1939.

The Battleship *USS Oregon* was towed from its berth next to the Broadway Bridge and placed in Battleship Oregon Memorial Park in 1938, south of the Hawthorne Bridge.

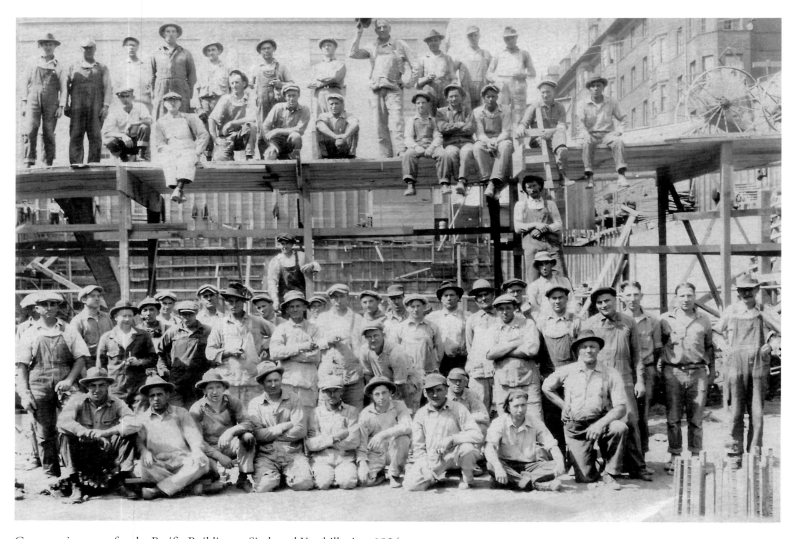

Construction crew for the Pacific Building at Sixth and Yamhill, circa 1924

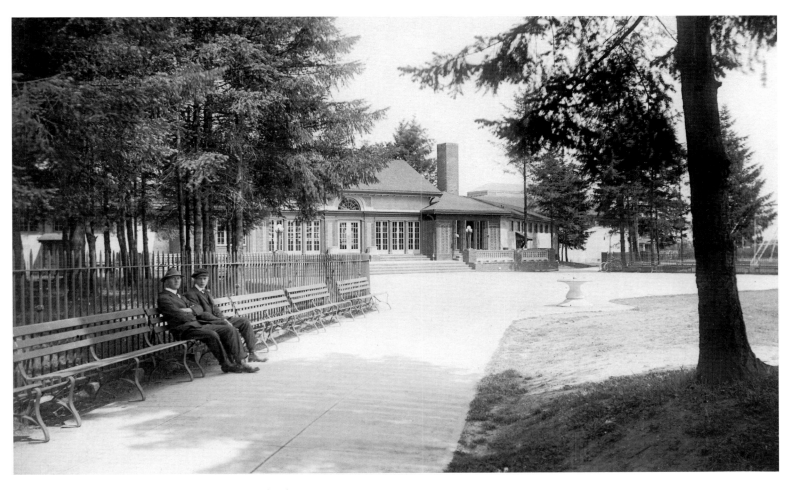

Peninsula Park Community House in North Portland in 1921

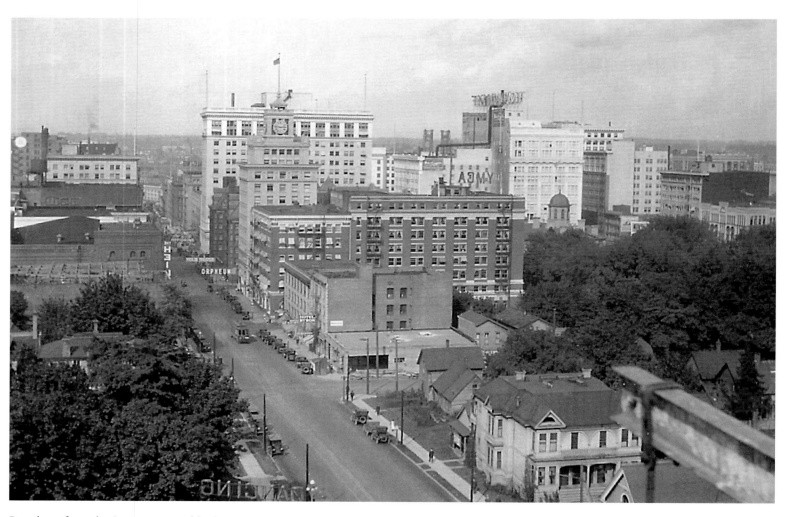

Broadway from the Sovereign Hotel looking North, circa 1923. There were still a few old residences left in the downtown area.

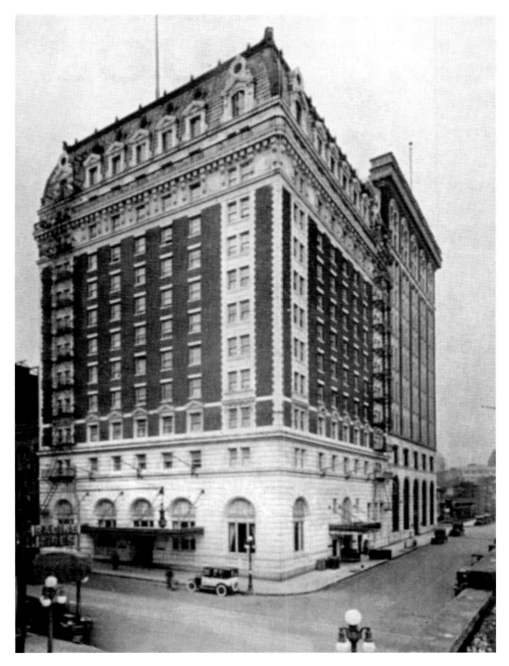

Lumberman Simon Benson's Hotel, circa 1924. Benson donated water fountains to the city in 1913, so when his lumber crews came into town they did not have to go into a saloon to get a drink of water.

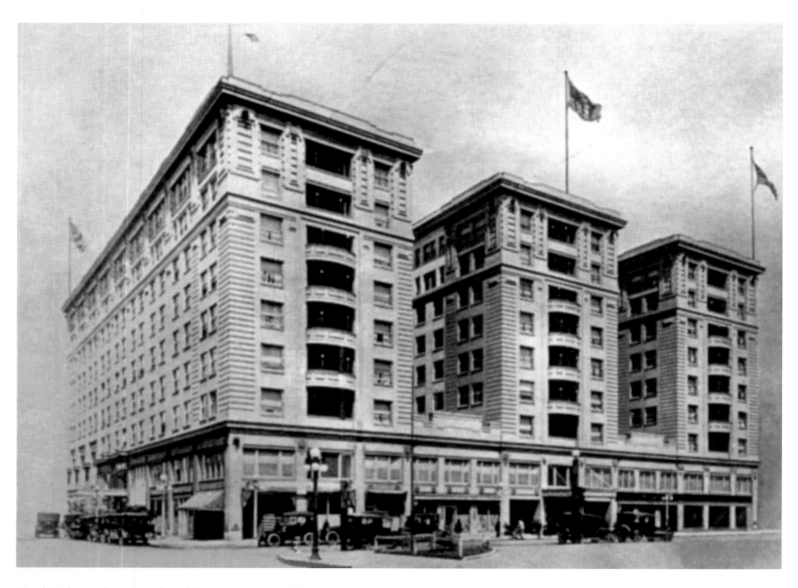

Hotel Multnomah on Fourth and Pine streets, circa 1924

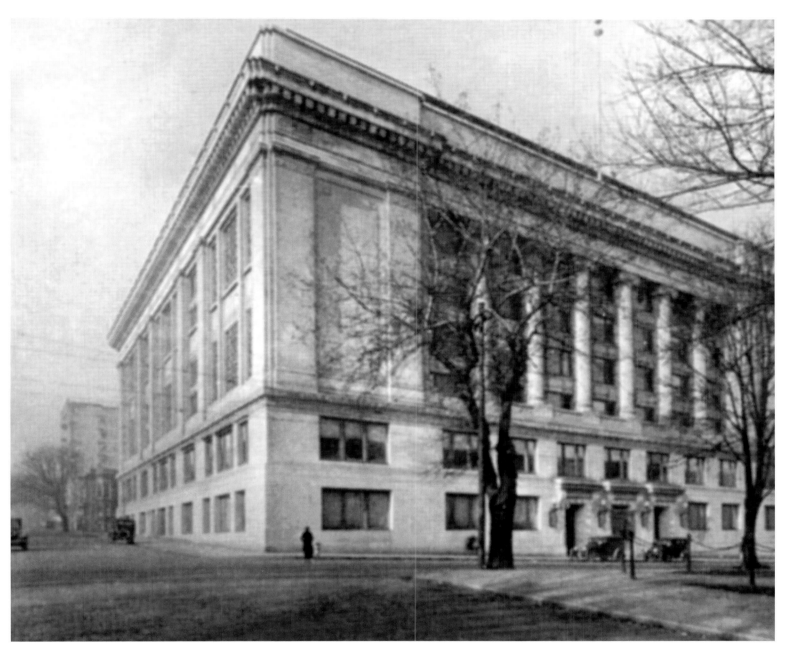

Multnomah County Courthouse on Fourth and Main streets, circa 1924

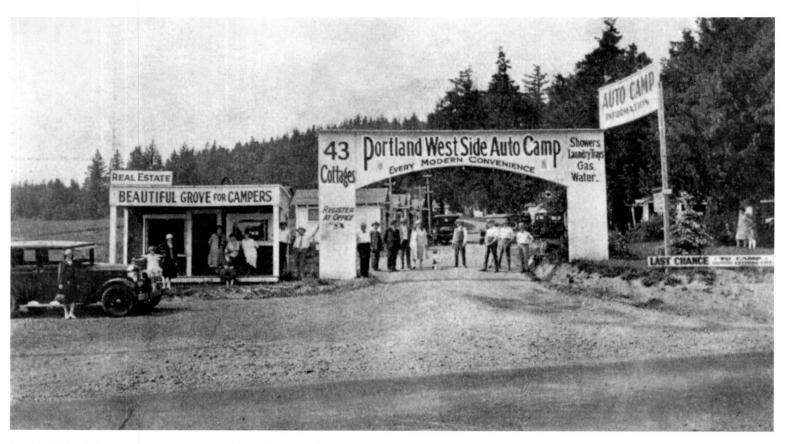

Portland Westside Auto Camp, circa 1925, located on Terwilliger Boulevard

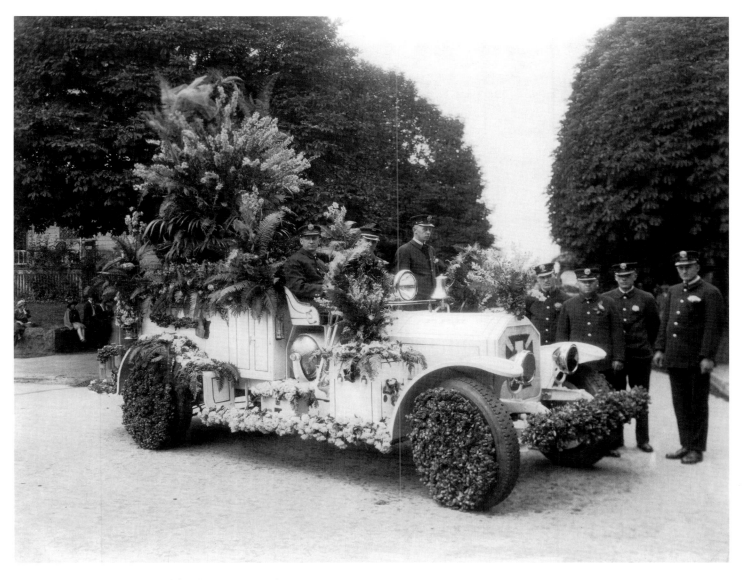

Fire Rescue Squad 1 decorated for the Rose Festival, circa 1926

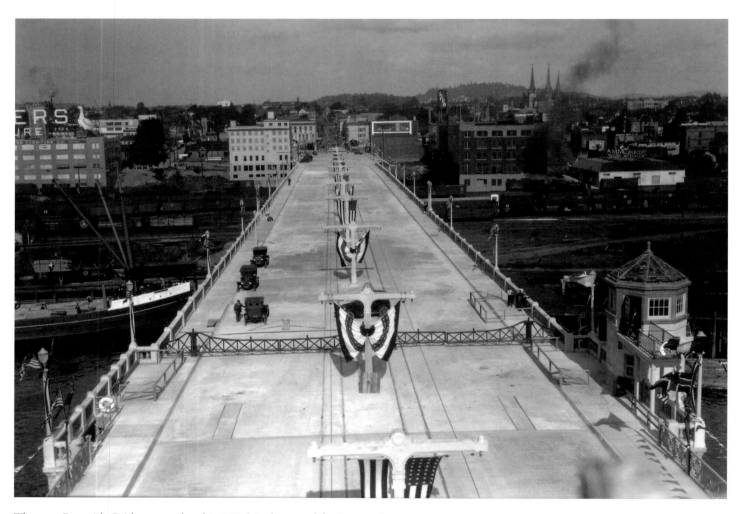

The new Burnside Bridge, completed in 1926, is decorated for its opening.

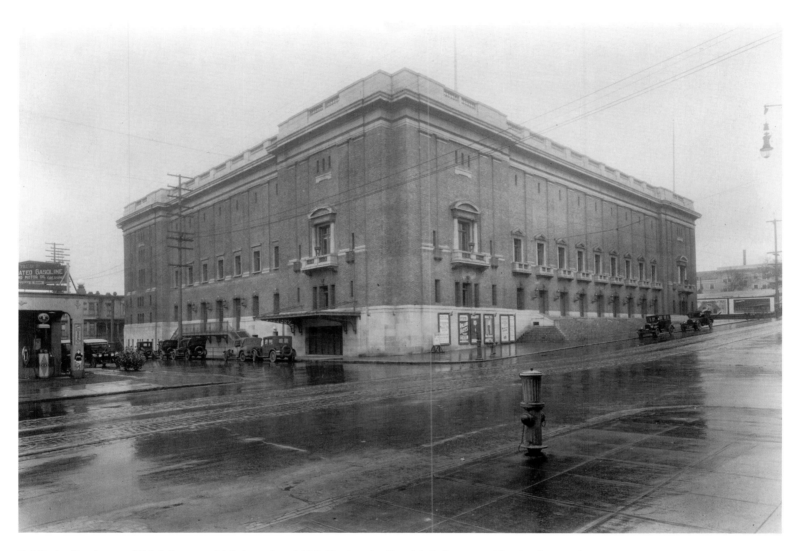

Public Auditorium on Third Street and Market, circa 1926. During the Spanish Influenza epidemic of 1918 the year-old auditorium was put to use as a temporary hospital. A poster advertises the appearance of humorist Will Rogers. It was rebuilt in the 1960s and renamed the Civic Auditorium. Today it is known as Keller Auditorium.

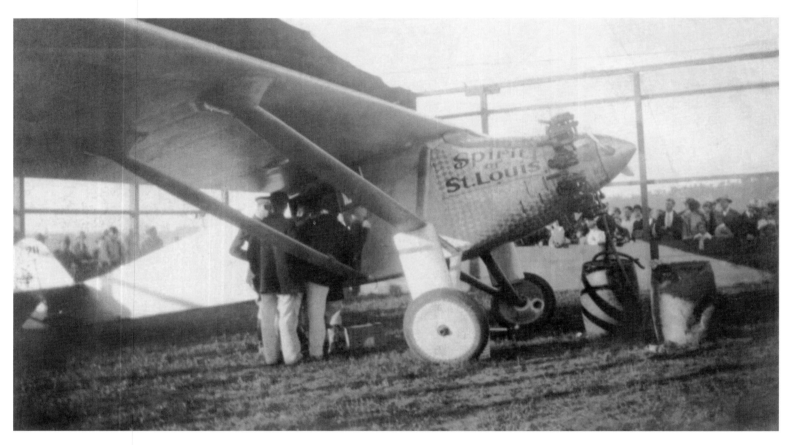

Aviator Charles A. Lindbergh was in Portland to promote commercial aviation. His airplane, the *Spirit of St. Louis,* was on display at Swan Island Airport, September 14 and 15, 1927.

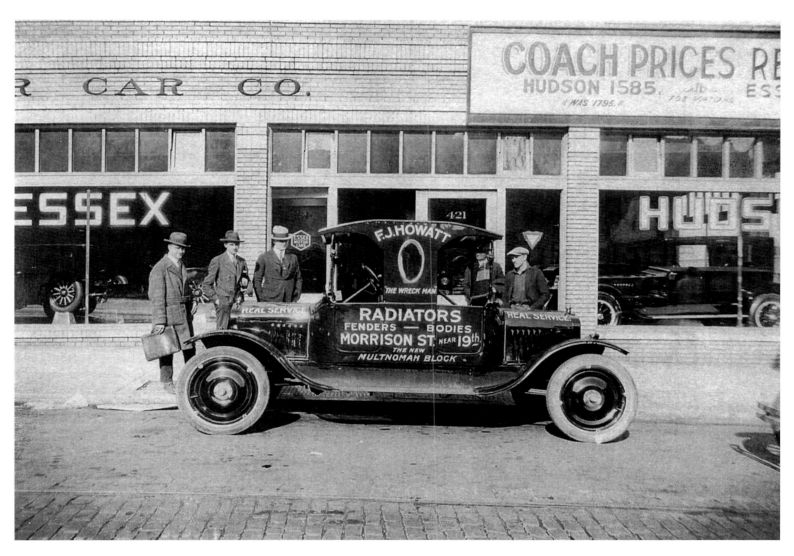

F. J. Howatt's Radiator Shop, in 1927, was in the new Multnomah Block on Morrison Street near Nineteenth Street. He advertised with this auto, "Headed both ways for Business."

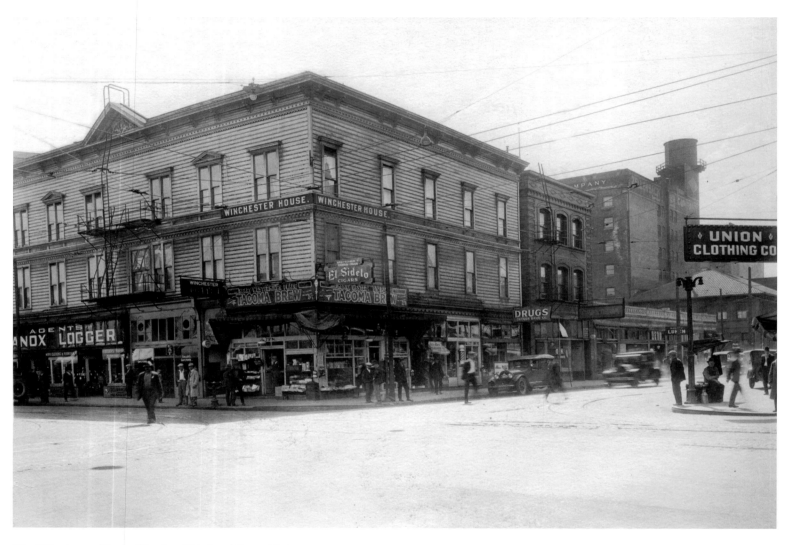

The Winchester House Hotel at Third and Burnside in 1928

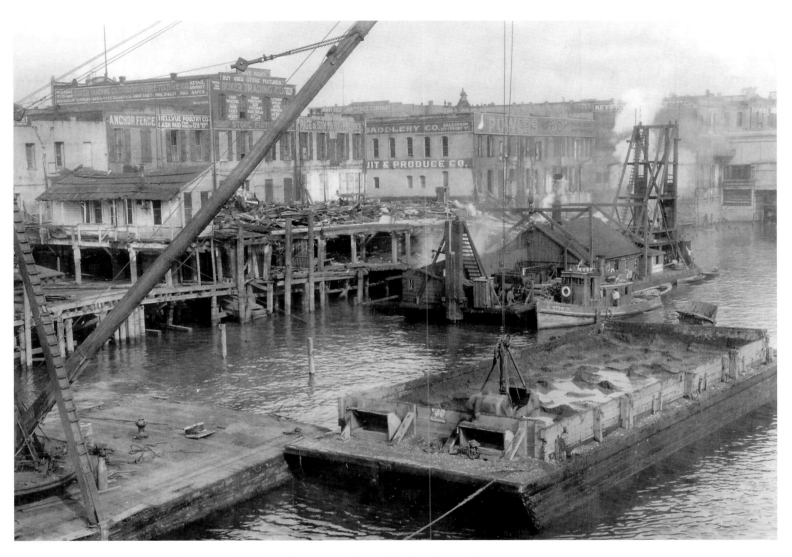

Dredging the Willamette River for the new harbor wall in 1928. The old docks will soon be removed.

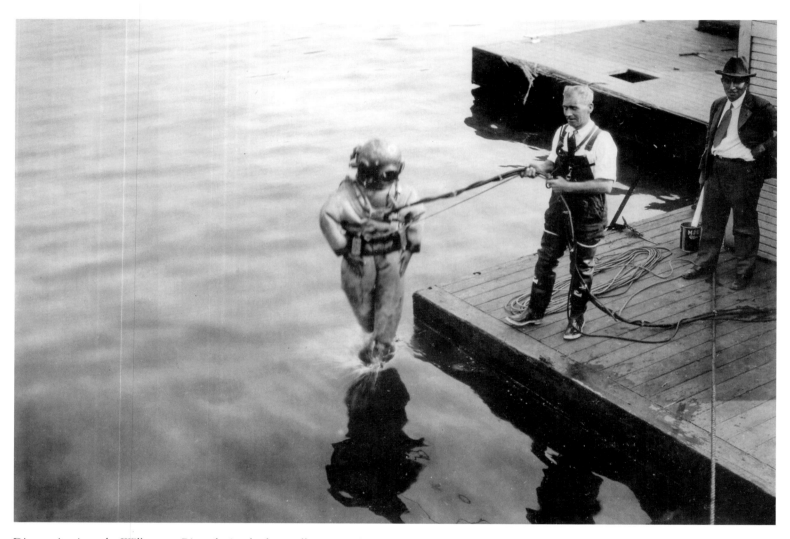

Diver going into the Willamette River during harbor wall construction in 1928

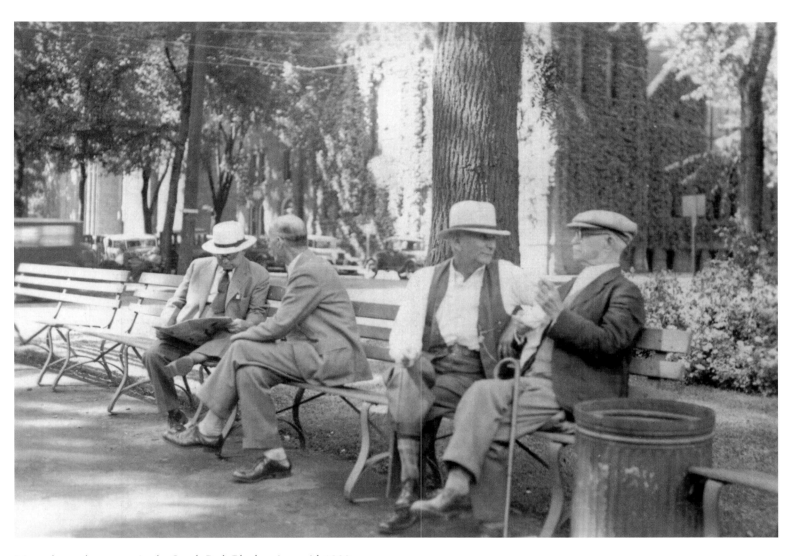

Men relax and converse in the South Park Blocks, circa mid-1930s.

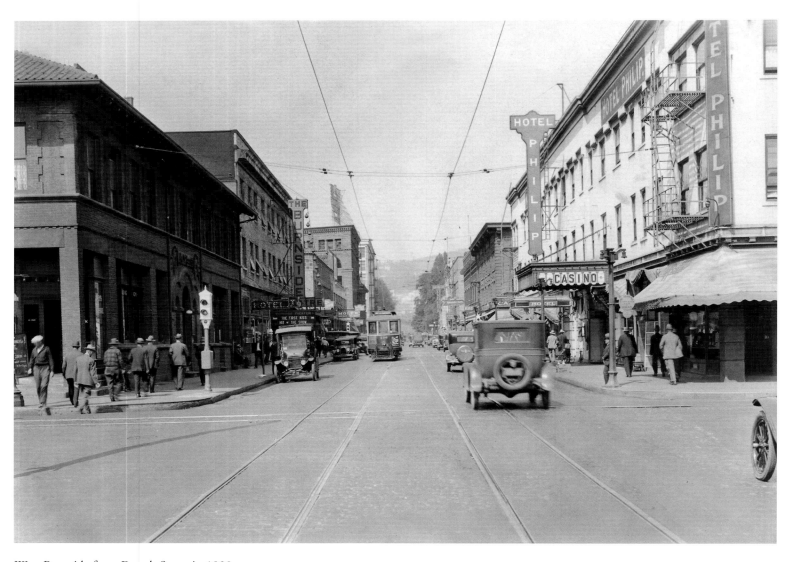

West Burnside from Fourth Street in 1930

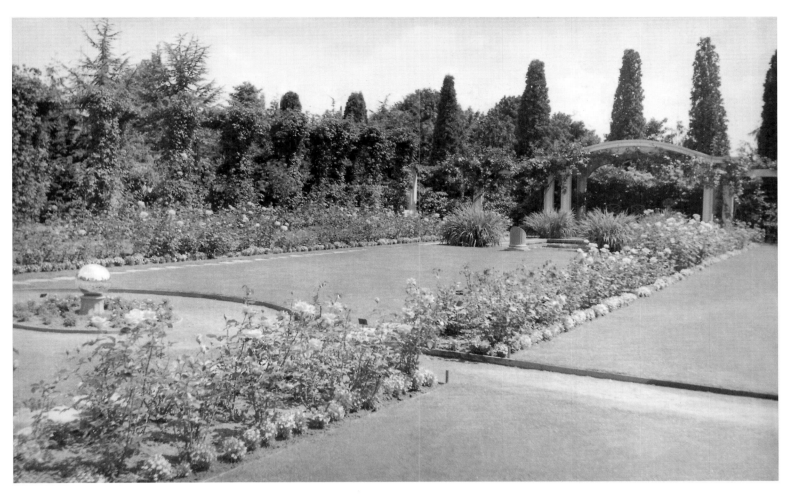

Lambert Gardens was a tourist attraction in Southeast Portland for decades, circa 1930s.

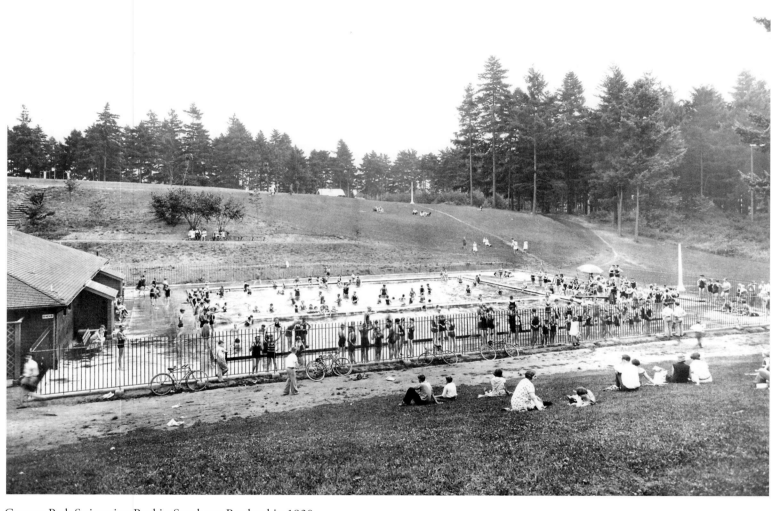

Creston Park Swimming Pool in Southeast Portland in 1930

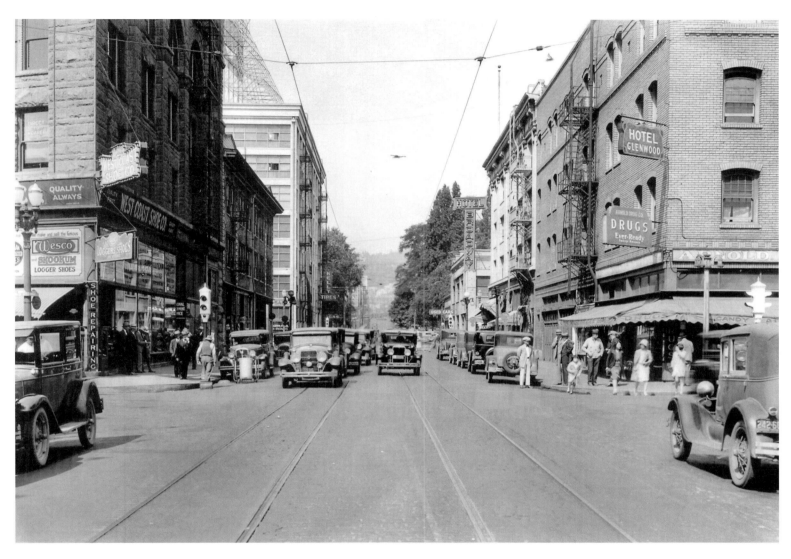

West Burnside at Sixth Street

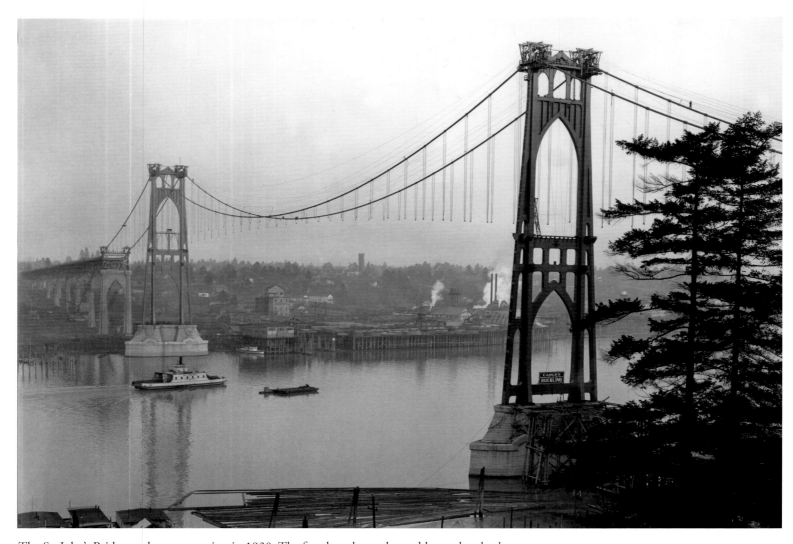

The St. John's Bridge under construction in 1930. The ferryboat beneath would soon be obsolete.

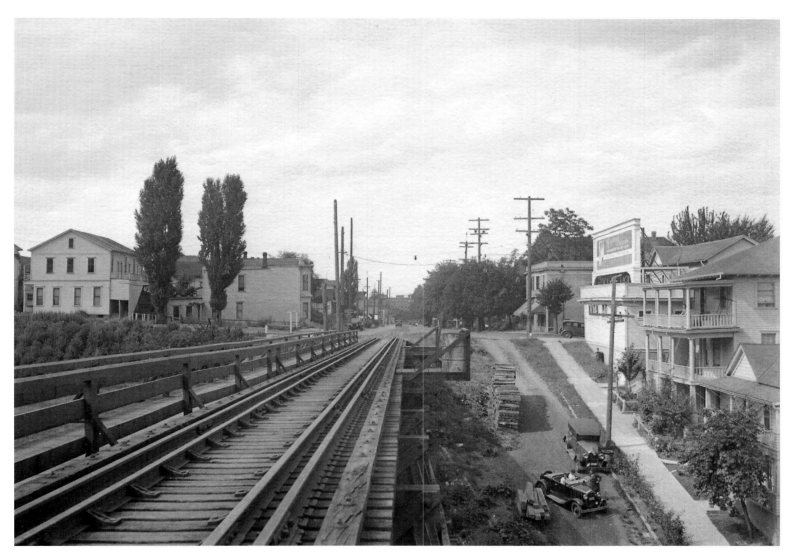

Fourth Street trestle in Southwest Portland in 1931, shortly before its removal

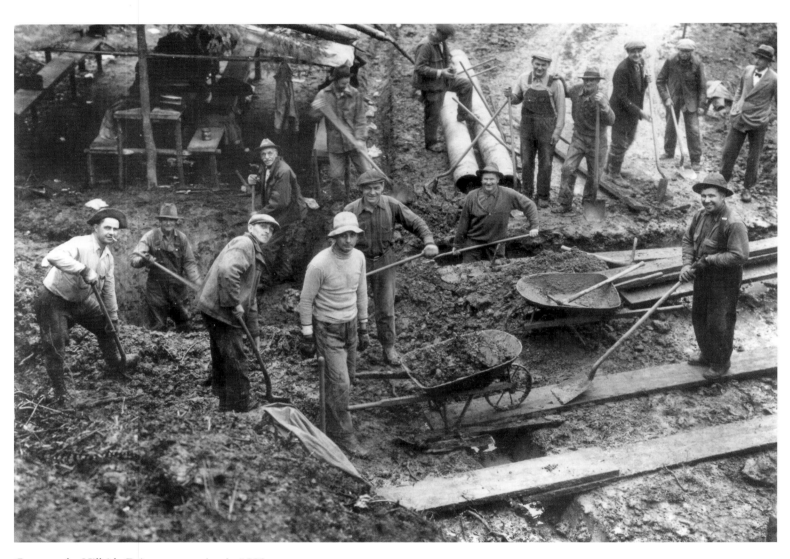

Crews at the Hillside Drive construction in 1932

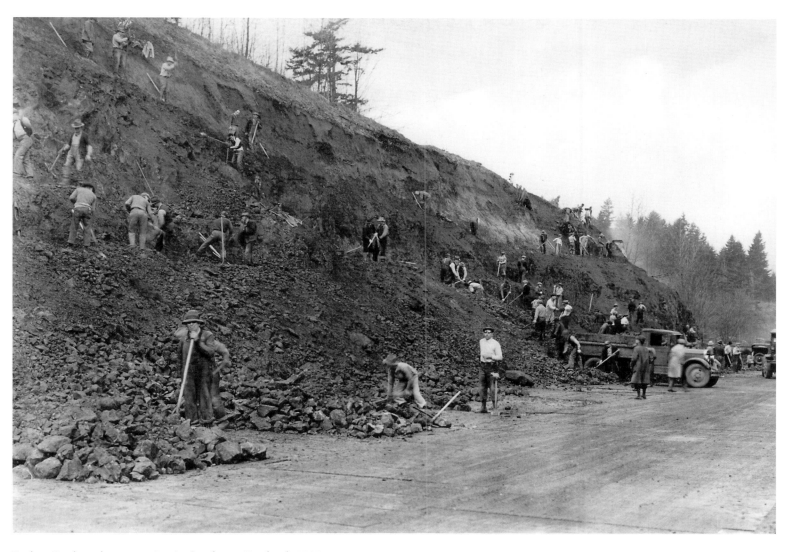

Barbur Boulevard construction in Southwest Portland, 1933

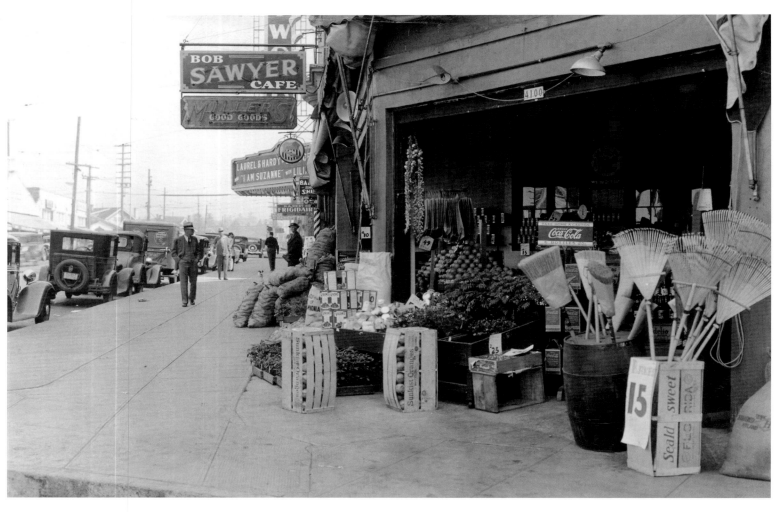

Market at NE 41st and Sandy Boulevard in 1934

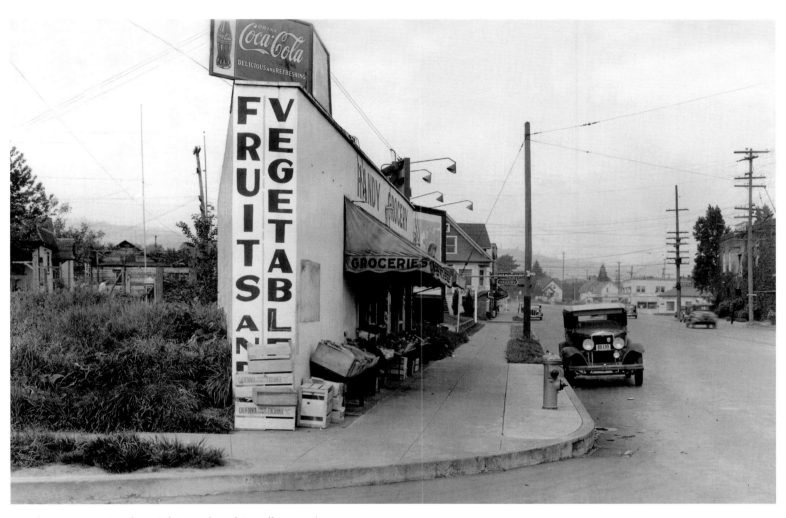

Handy Grocery at Southeast Thirteenth and Powell in 1934

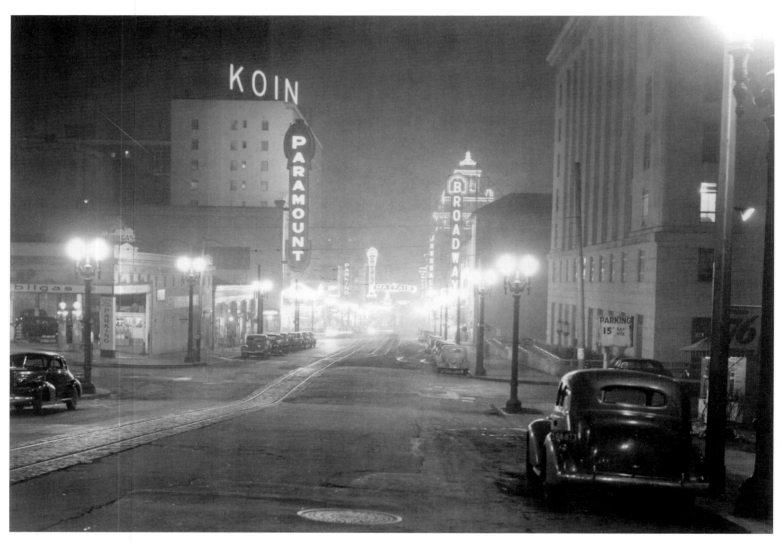

Night view of Southwest Broadway showing illuminated signs of the Broadway and
Paramount theaters. Also shown is the sign for radio station KOIN, which had its studios
in the new Heathman Hotel. Circa 1935

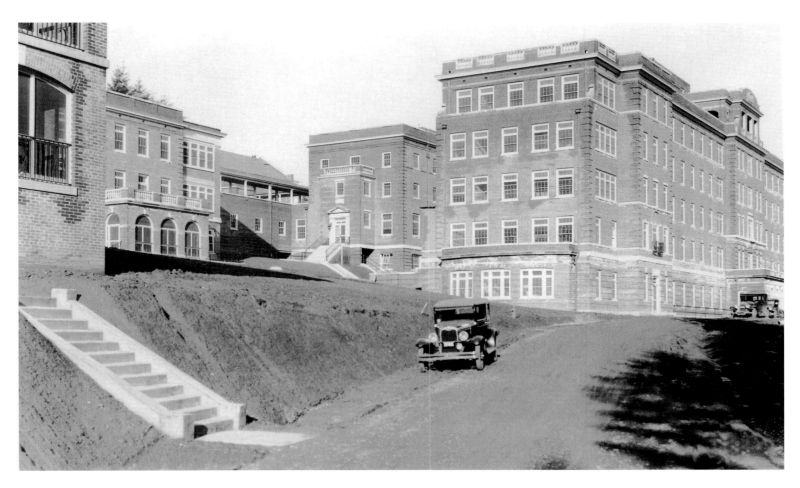

U.S. Veterans Hospital on Marquam Hill in Southwest Portland, circa 1935

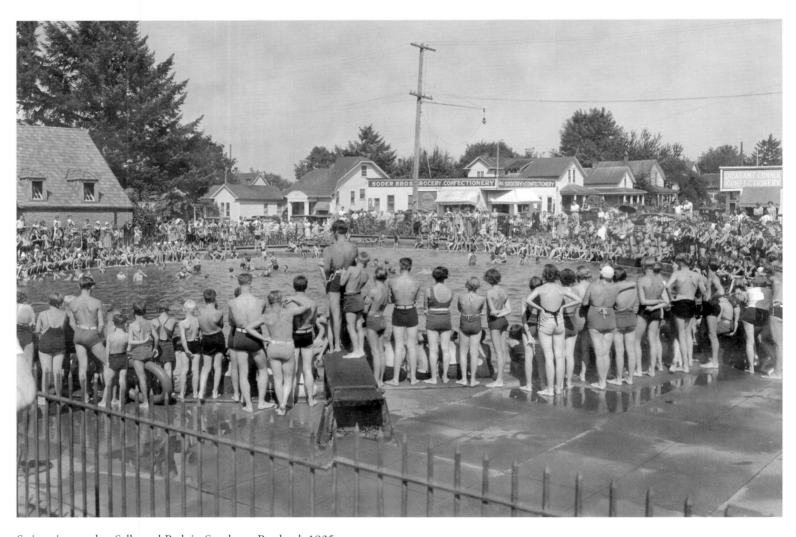

Swimming pool at Sellwood Park in Southeast Portland, 1935

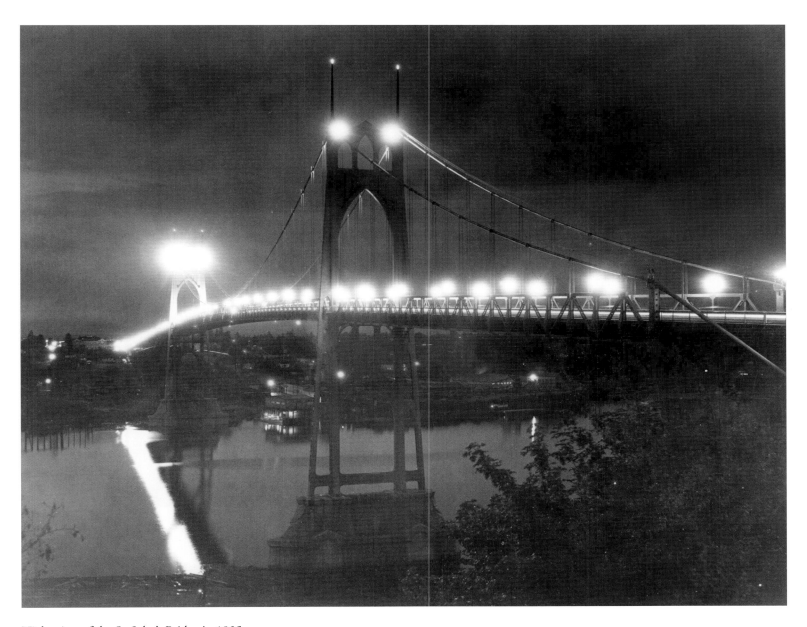

Night view of the St. John's Bridge in 1935

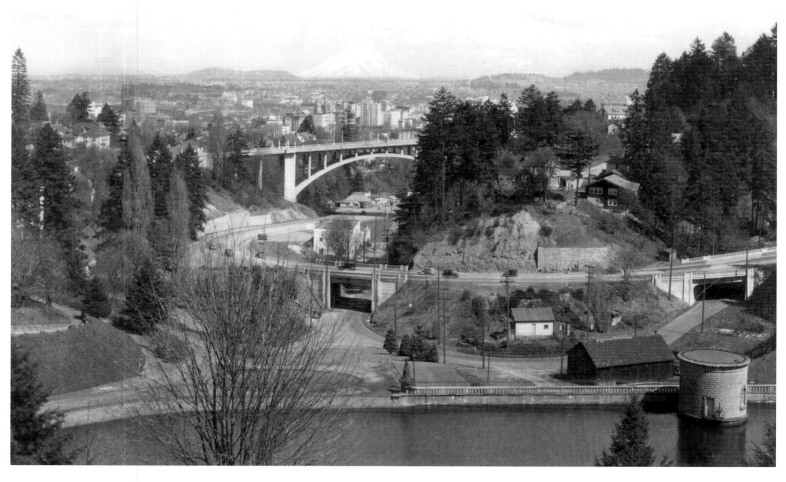

Vista Avenue Bridge and Reservoir 4 from Washington Park, circa 1935. The Jefferson Street entrance to
Canyon Road curves under the Vista Avenue Bridge.

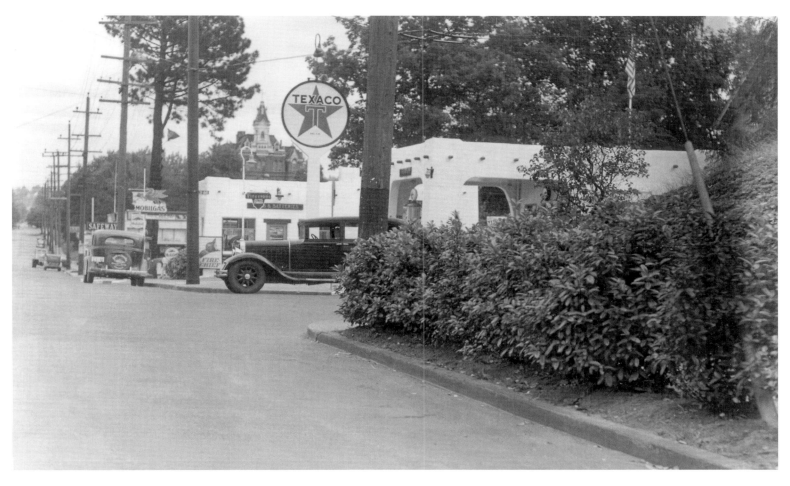

Southeast 28th and Stark circa 1937. In the background is the Mt. St. Joseph Home for the Aged, which was built in the 1890s as Portland Hospital.

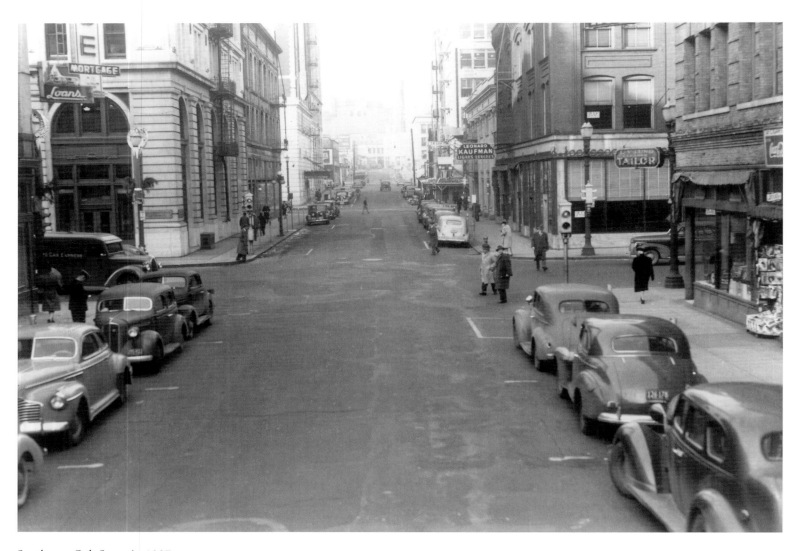

Southwest Oak Street in 1937

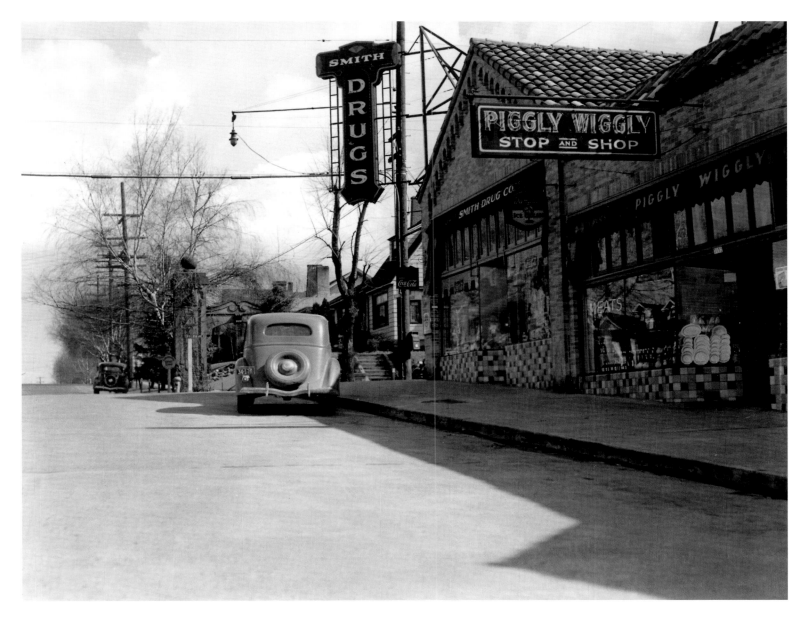

The Piggly Wiggly Stop and Shop grocery store at Southeast 32nd and Burnside in 1937

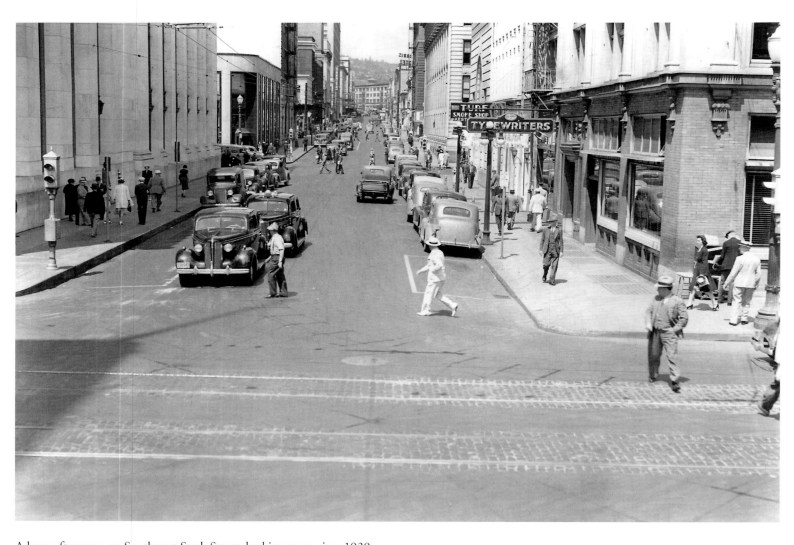

A busy afternoon on Southwest Stark Street, looking west, circa 1939

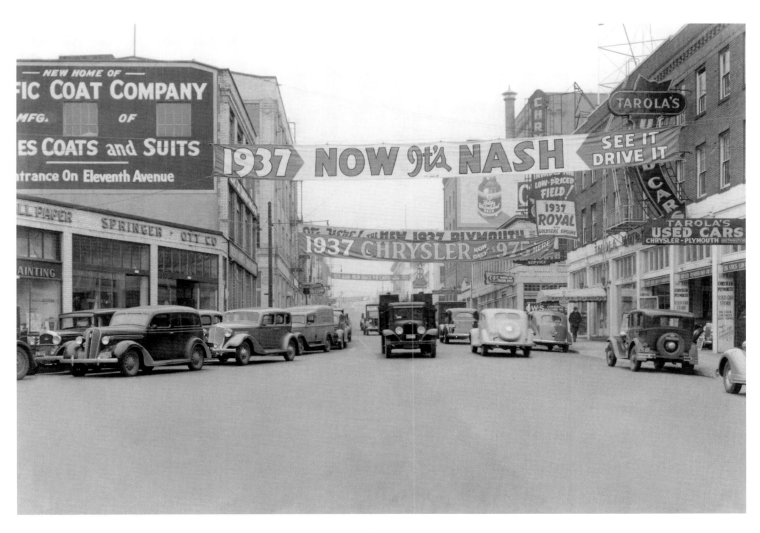

Auto Row on West Burnside in 1937

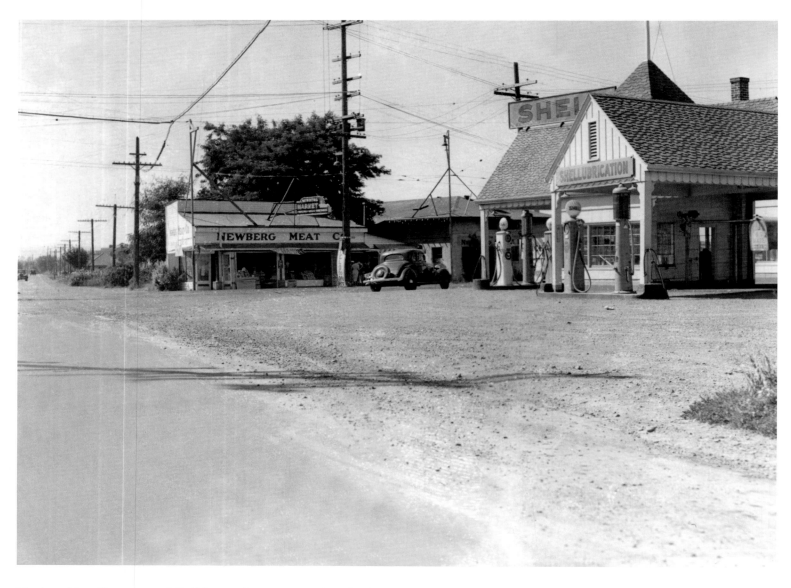

Newberg Meat Company and Shell Service Station on North Columbia Boulevard in 1937

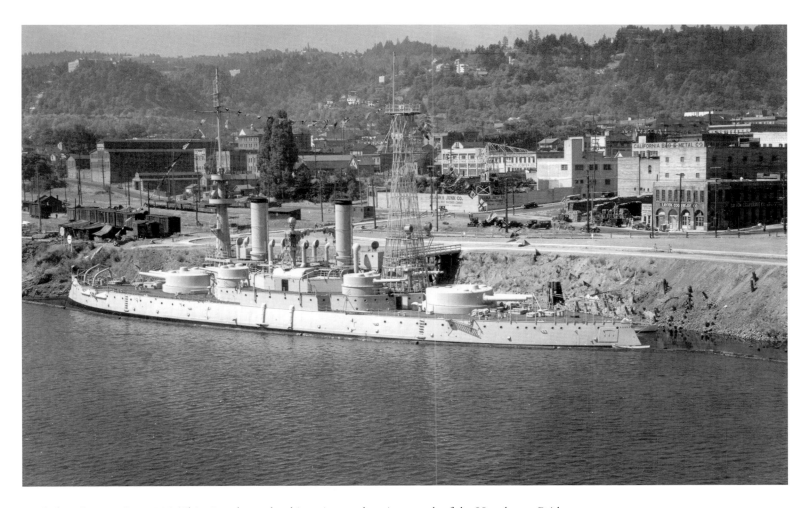

Battleship *Oregon,* circa 1938. This view shows the ship at its new location, south of the Hawthorne Bridge that was developed into Battleship Oregon Memorial Park. The ship was relinquished to the government for scrap in 1942 and ended up as an ammunition barge. The mast was salvaged and today is part of the Battleship Oregon Memorial in Governor Tom McCall Waterfront Park.

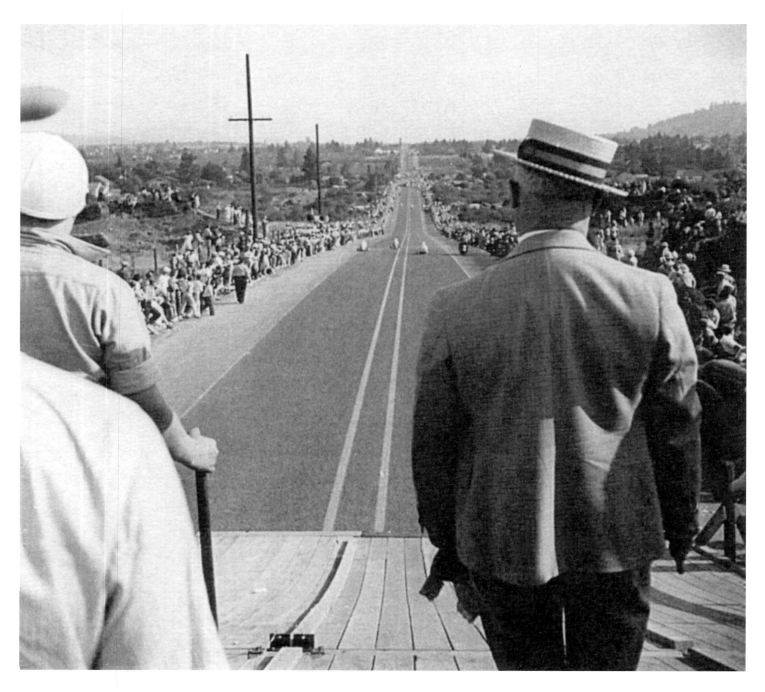

Looking south on Northeast 82nd from the 1938 Soapbox Derby starting line

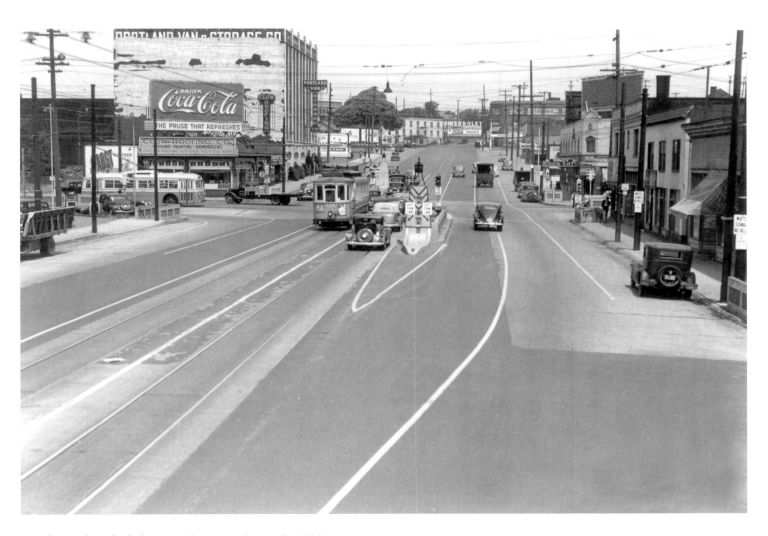

North Broadway looking east to Interstate Avenue in 1939

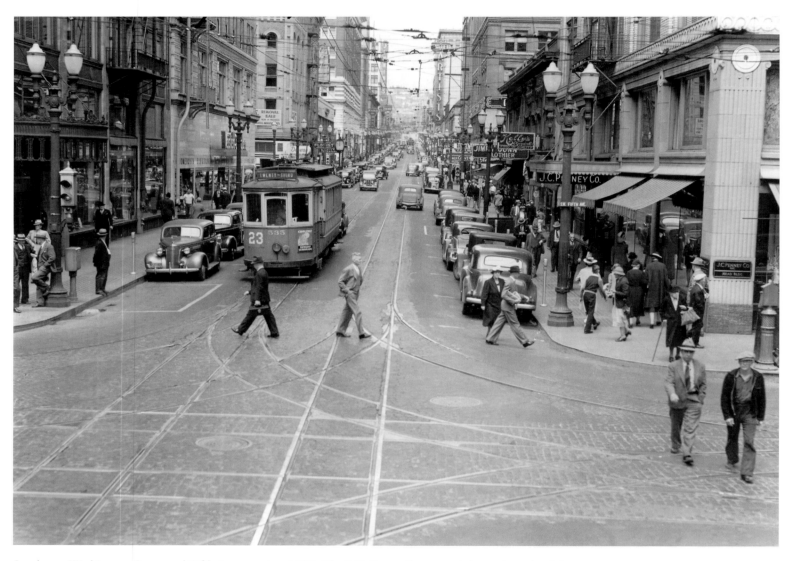

Southwest Washington Street and Fifth Avenue, circa 1939. The J.C. Penny Company is located on the right.

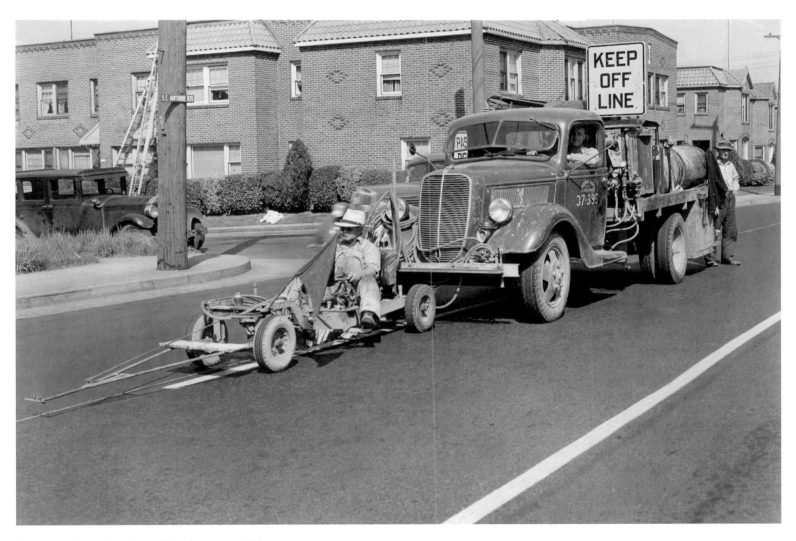

Street striping on Southeast Hawthorne in 1939

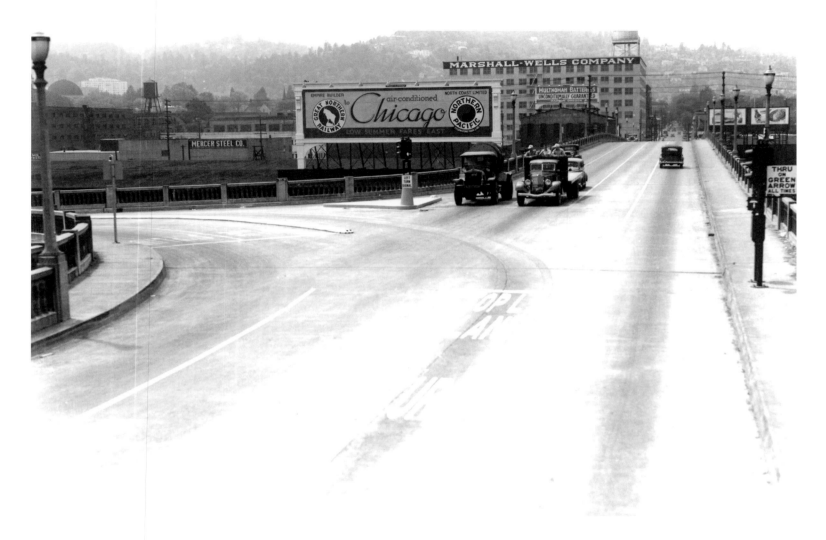

The Northwest Tenth Avenue connection to the Lovejoy Viaduct in 1939, which carried traffic over the railroad yards

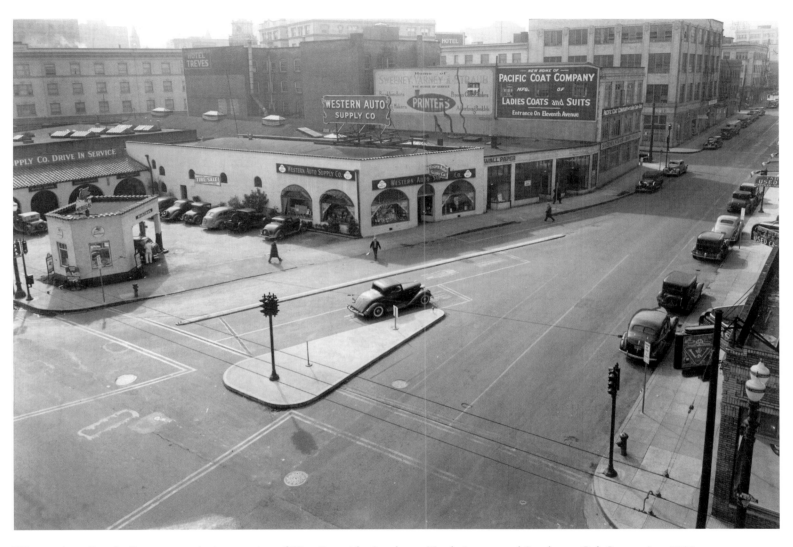

Western Auto Supply Company at the intersection of West Burnside, Southwest Tenth Avenue and Southwest Oak Street, circa 1939

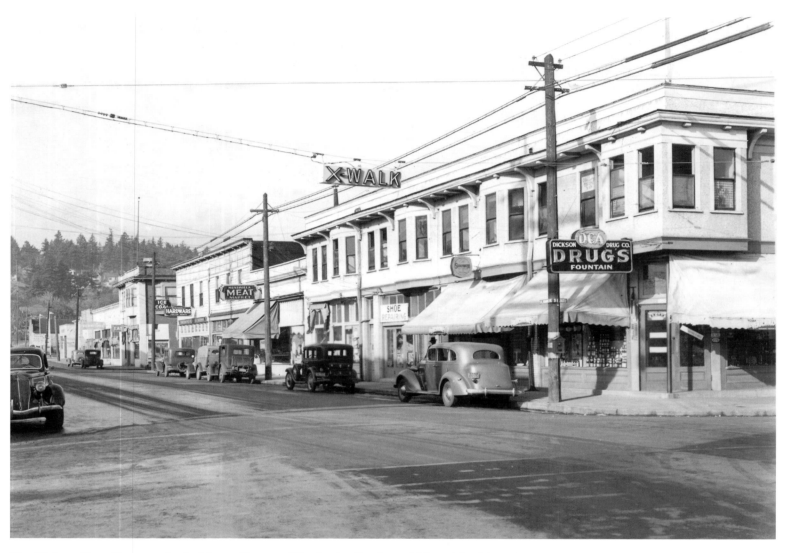

The Dickson Drug Company in the Montavilla area of Portland at Southeast 80th and Stark in 1939

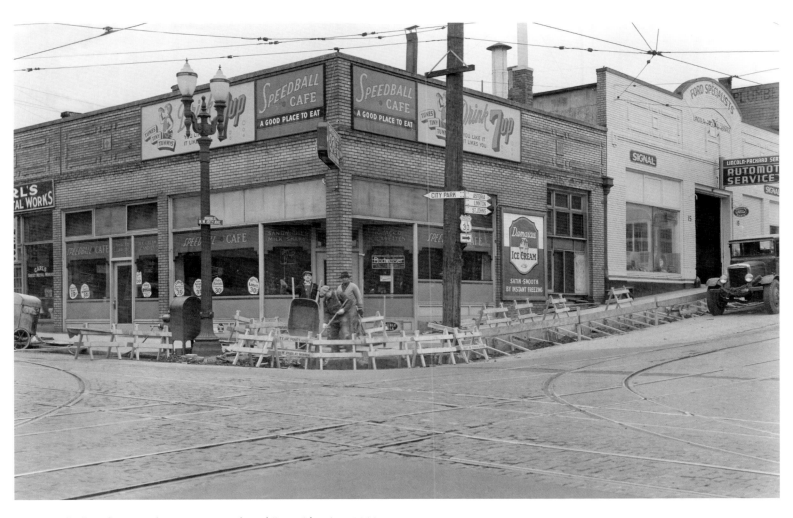

The Speedball Cafe at Northwest Nineteenth and Burnside, circa 1939

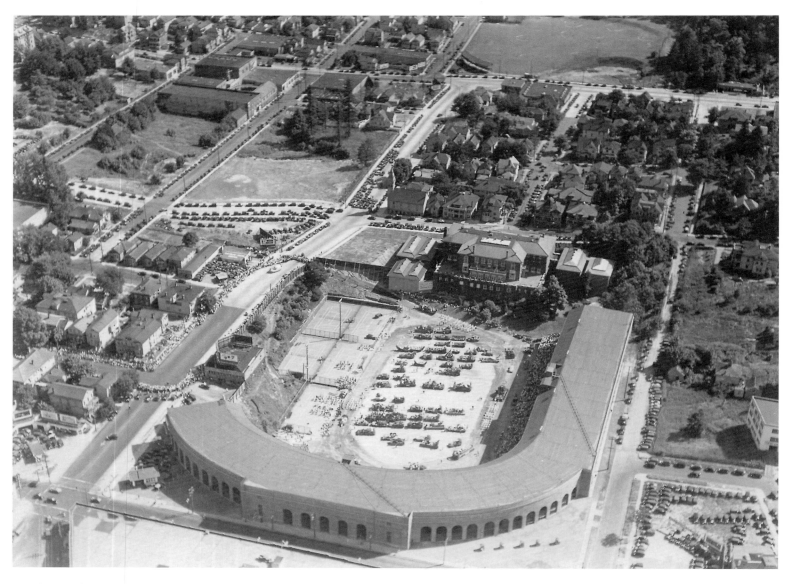

Aerial view of the Multnomah Athletic Club and Stadium, circa 1939

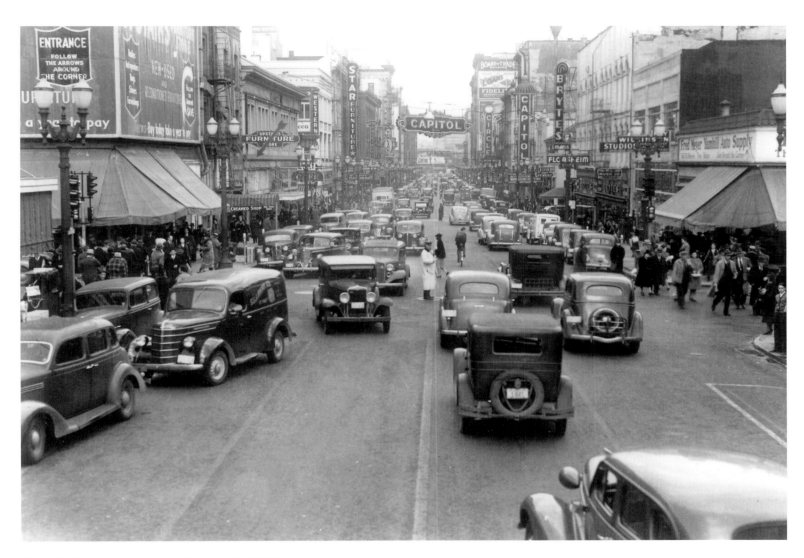

View of a busy Southwest Fourth Avenue in 1940

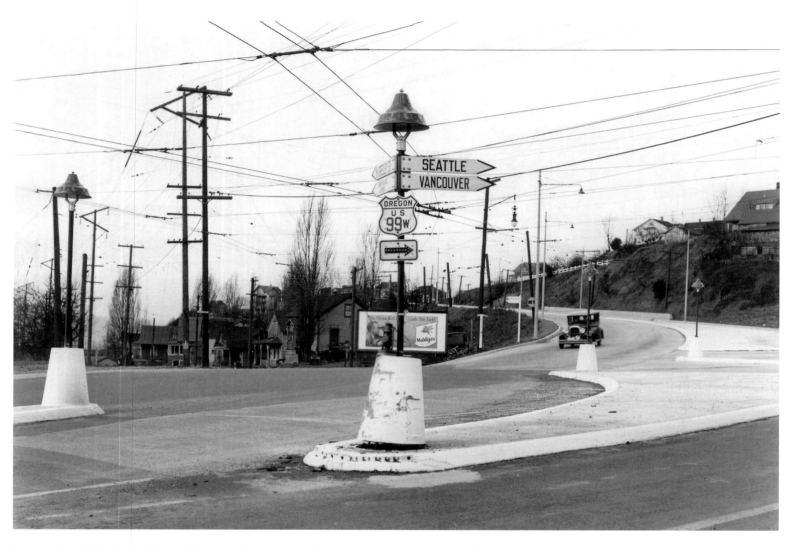

Intersection of North Greeley and Interstate Avenue in 1940. Interstate Avenue was part of U.S. Highway 99W.

From 1940 to a Modern City

1940–1970s

World War II brought defense work into the city, increasing the population. Women entered the workforce. The former Swan Island Airport was transformed into a Kaiser Shipyard in 1942 and became an industrial area after the war.

Vanport, built as a city of homes for shipyard workers, was inundated by floodwaters of the Columbia River in 1948. Vanport College, today's Portland State University, was displaced by the flood, moving to a former shipyard building in St. Johns, and finally to the former Lincoln High School building facing the South Park Blocks in 1952.

The Portland Hotel was torn down in 1951 and was replaced by the Meier and Frank parking lot.

Dependence upon the automobile led to the removal of several blocks of old historic buildings on the waterfront for the development of the Harbor Drive highway in the early 1940s. A freeway system, which started in the 1950s, completed a loop around the city when the Fremont Bridge opened in 1973.

Destruction of many old buildings led to historic preservation efforts in the late 1960s and 1970s. The downtown area continued to be reinvented as old buildings were replaced with full-block structures. As the 1970s came to an end, plans had been formulated to replace the Meier and Frank parking lot with what became today's Pioneer Courthouse Square.

Portland, like many cities, had war protests, racial unrest, and environmental concerns in the 1960s and 1970s. The city continued to develop socially to accommodate the needs of a growing, diverse community.

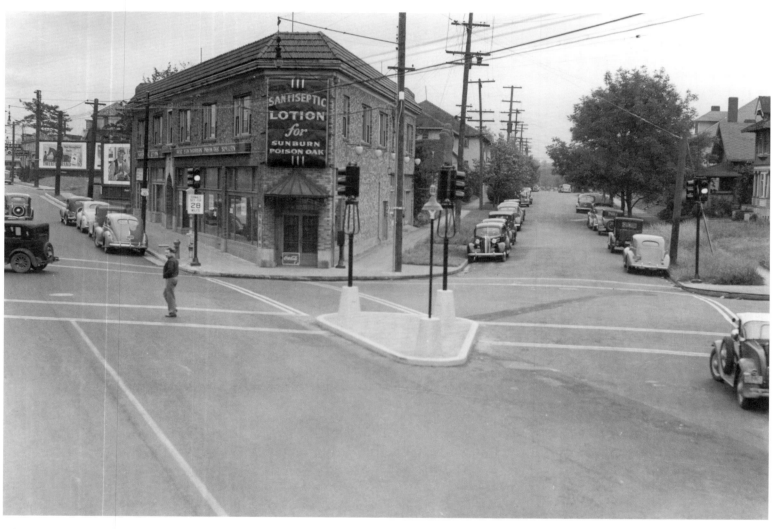

The Santiseptic Company was located in the Schefter Building at Northeast Twentieth and Sandy Boulevard in this view from 1940.

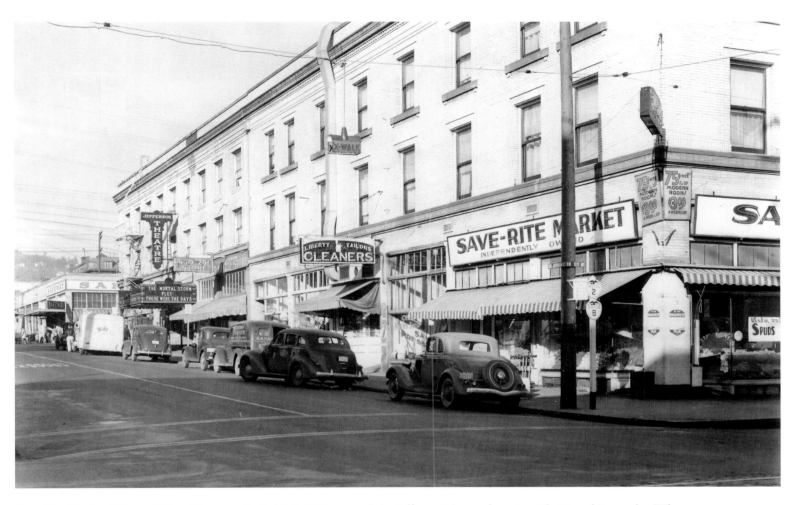

Save-Rite Market, Liberty Tailors Cleaners, the 5, 10 & 25 Store, and the Jefferson Theatre featuring *The Mortal Storm* plus "Those Were the Days," can be seen in this view of Southwest Jefferson at Eleventh, circa 1940.

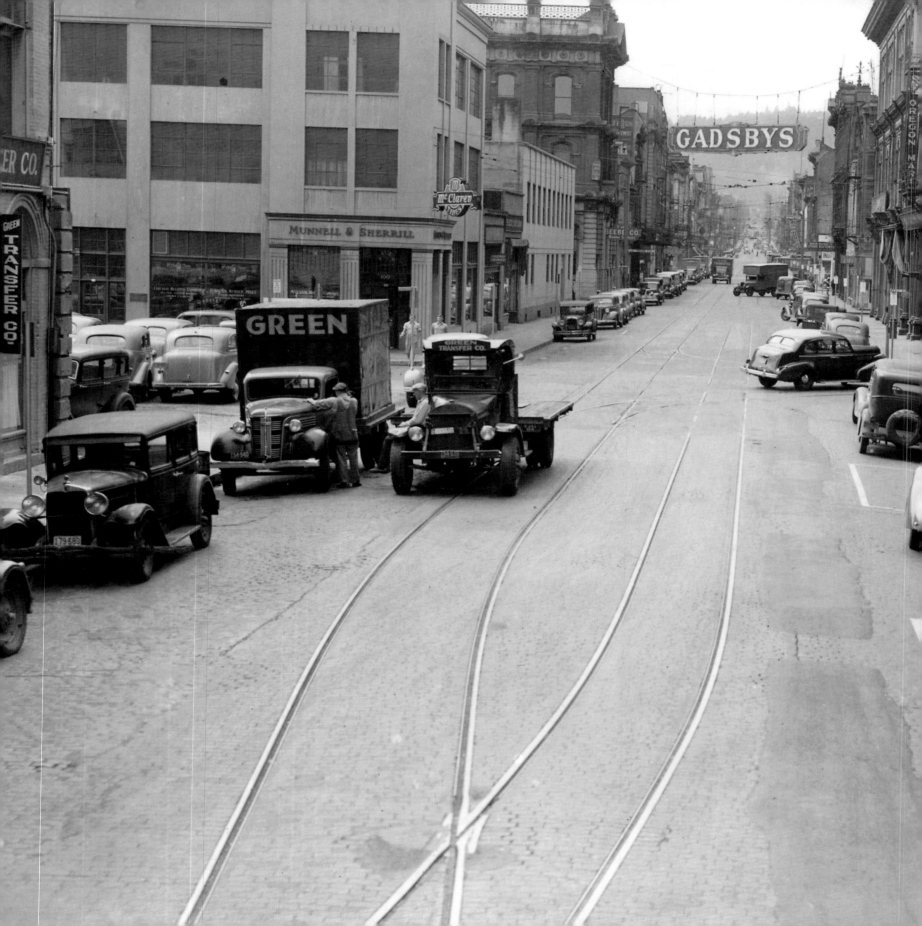

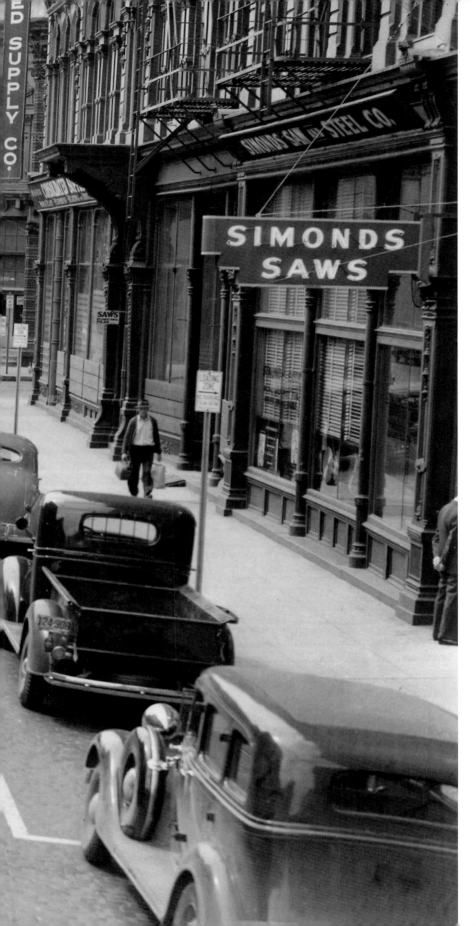

Southwest First Avenue in 1940

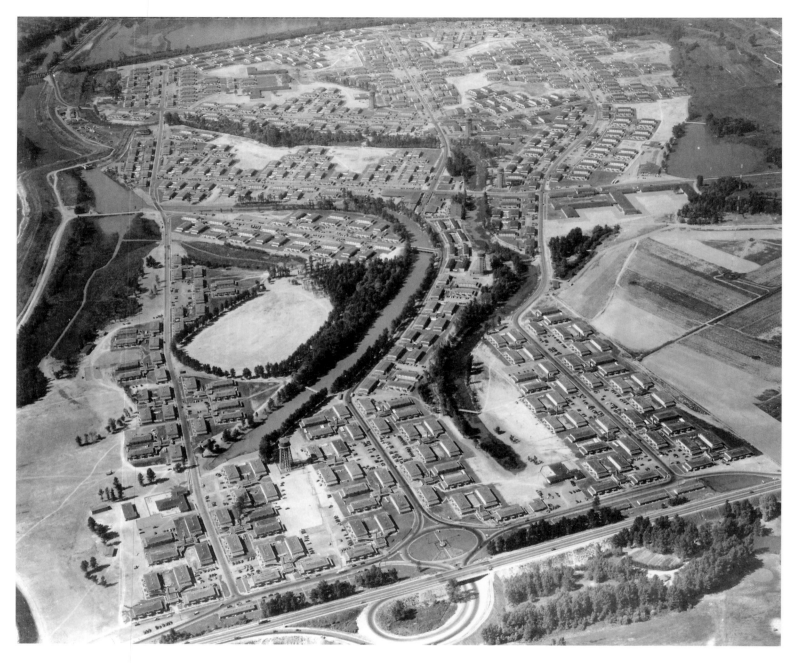

Vanport City, seen in this aerial view from 1943, was a planned community built for shipyard workers.

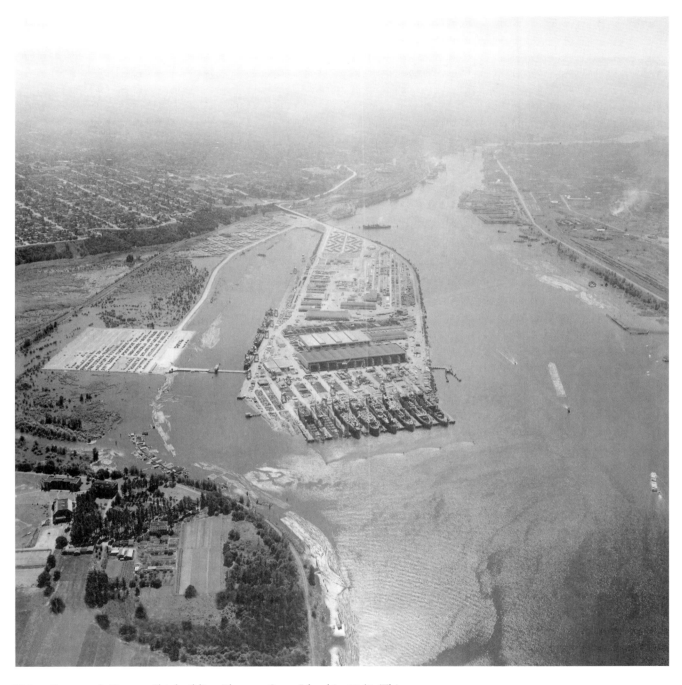

Kaiser Company's Oregon Shipbuilding Plant on Swan Island in 1943. This
location had previously been the site of the Swan Island Airport.

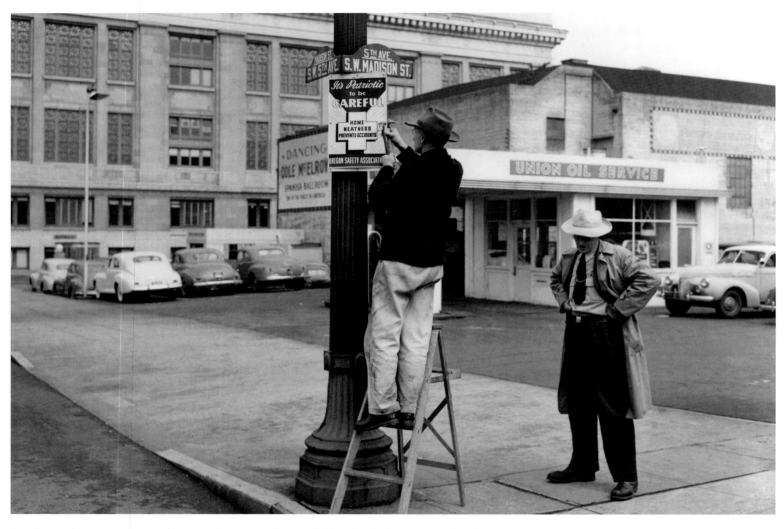

Gentleman hanging a sign reading "It's Patriotic to be Careful" during Safety Week in 1944.

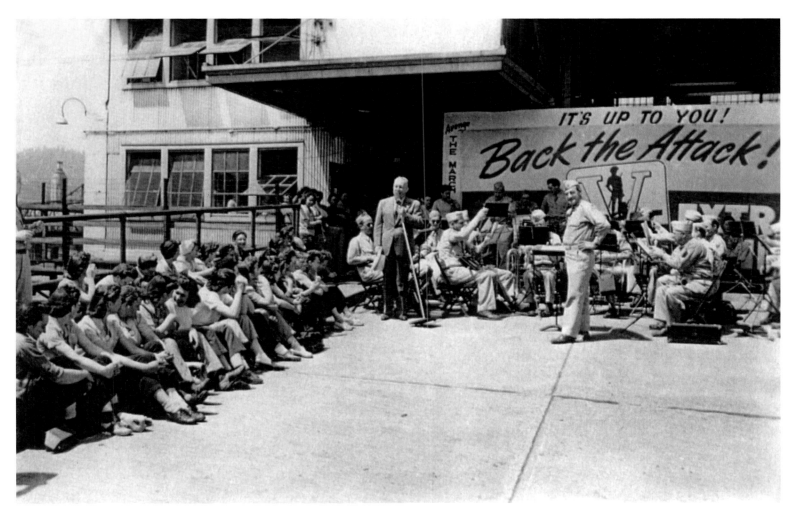

War bond rally at the Columbia Aircraft plant on the Portland eastside waterfront, circa 1944

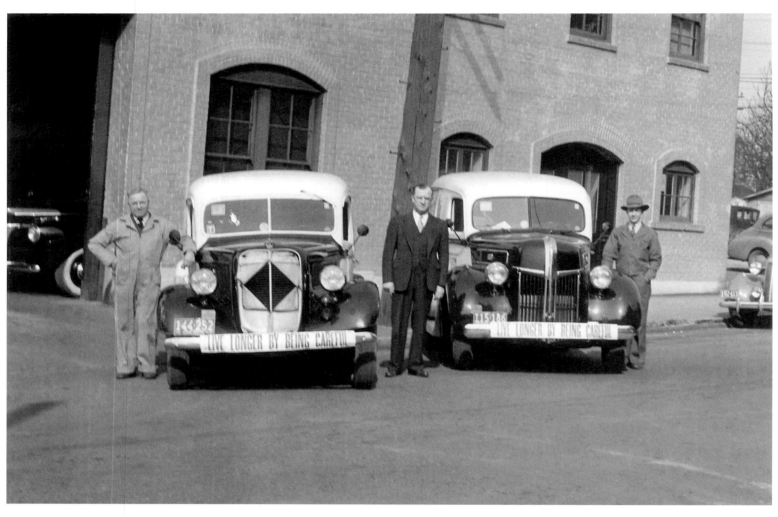

Safety bumper signs were attached to these city-owned vehicles during Safety Week in 1944.

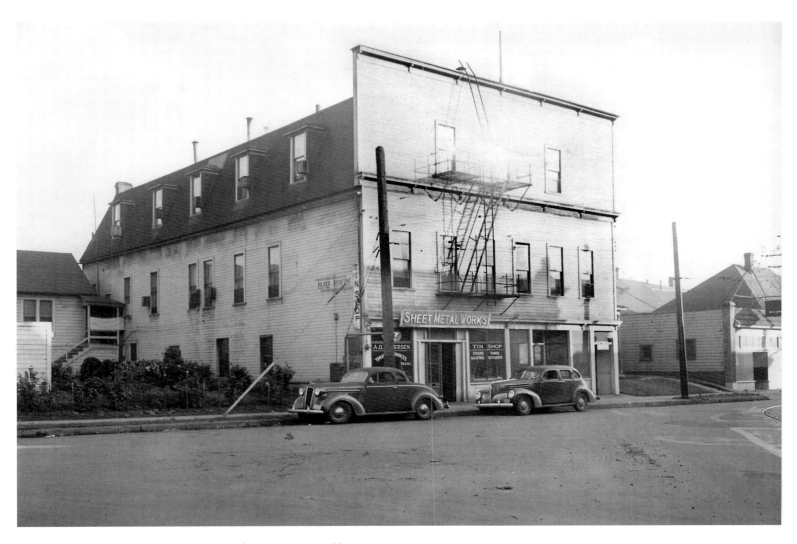

Sheet Metal Works building on North Larrabee Ave. circa 1944.

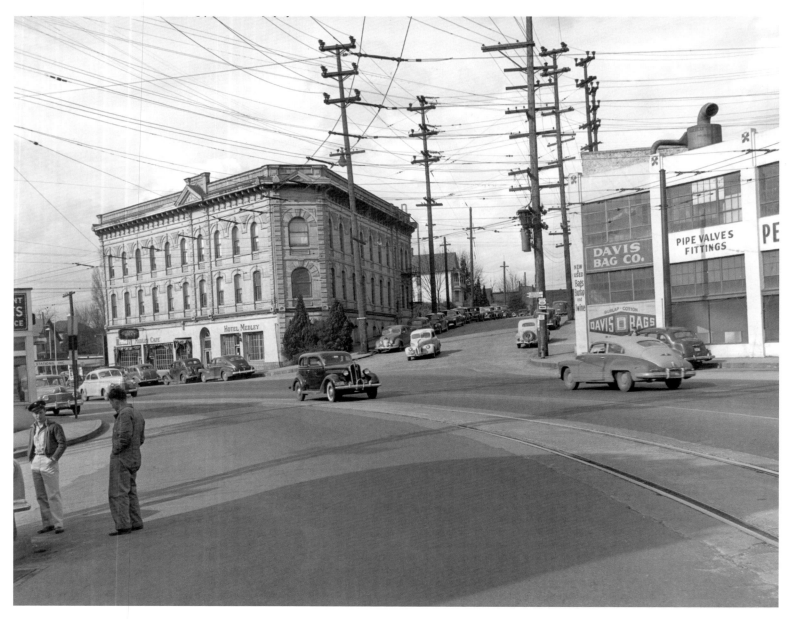

The Hotel Medley at North Interstate and Albina Avenues in 1945

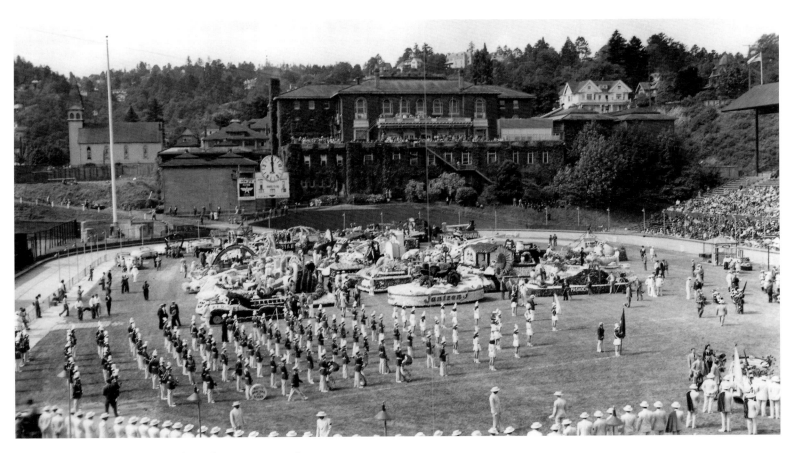

Rose Festival floats at Multnomah Stadium in June 1949

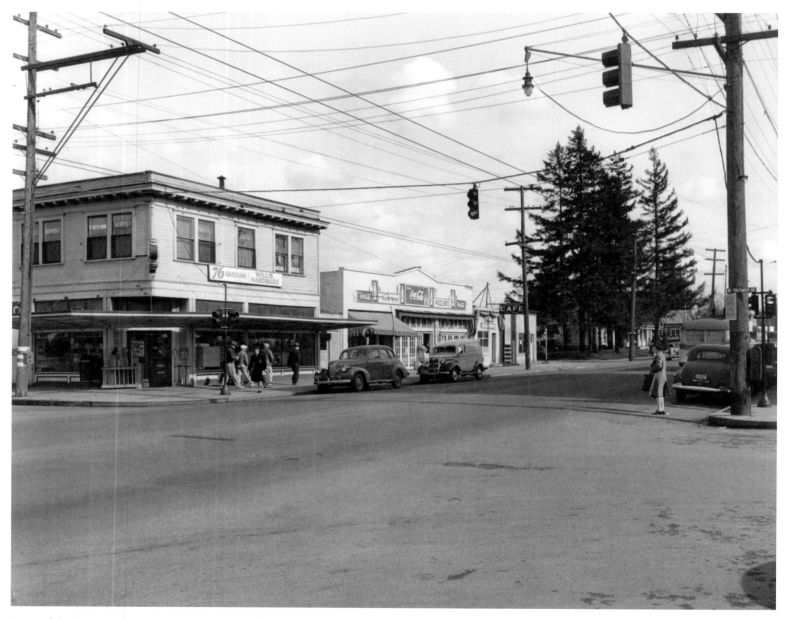

View of the intersection of North Lombard and Portsmouth in 1945

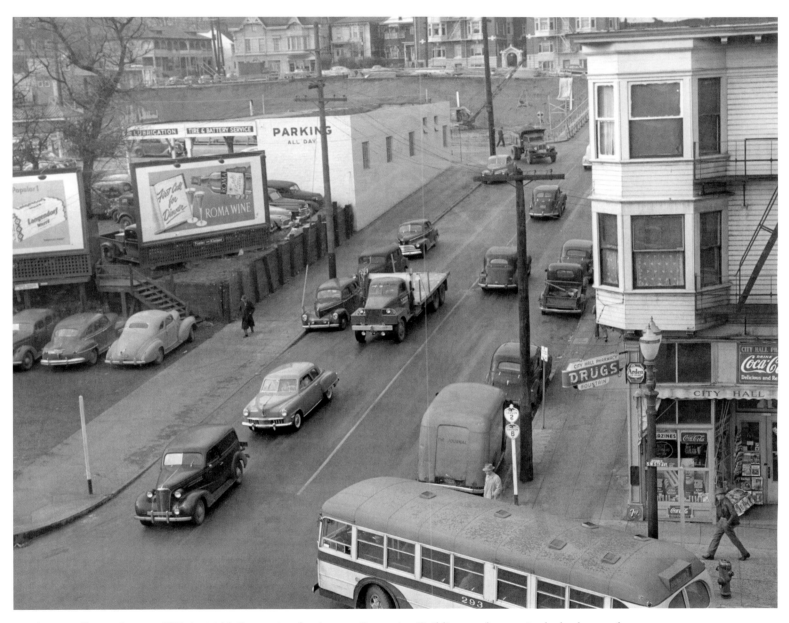

Southwest Jefferson Street at Fifth in 1946. Excavation for the new Oregonian Building can be seen in the background.

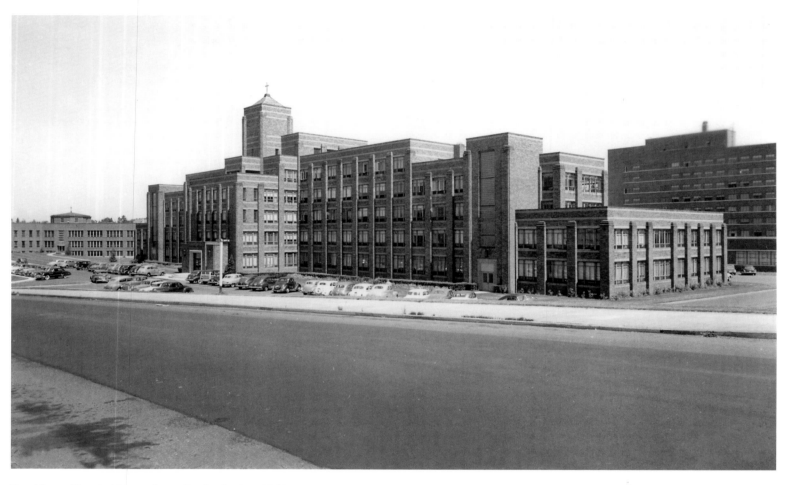

Providence Hospital in northeast Portland, circa 1948

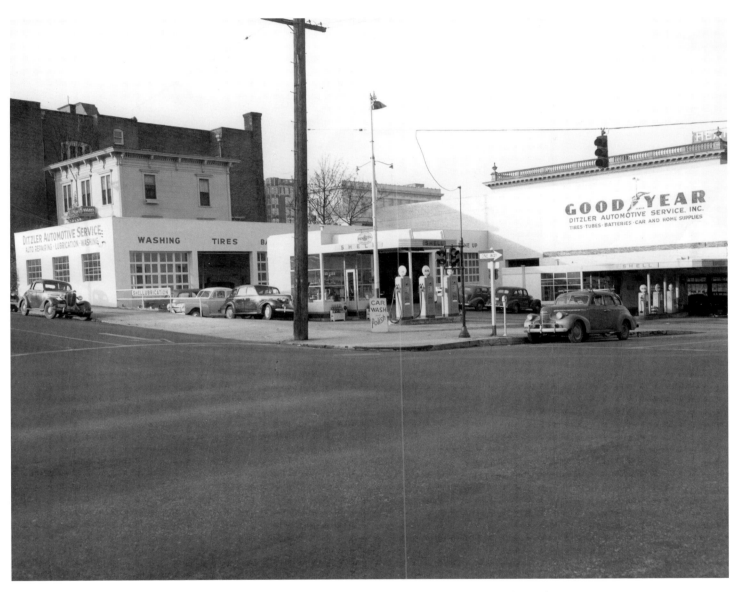

In 1948, a service station and tire store shared the block at Southwest Fourth Avenue and Columbia with an old house and a hotel.

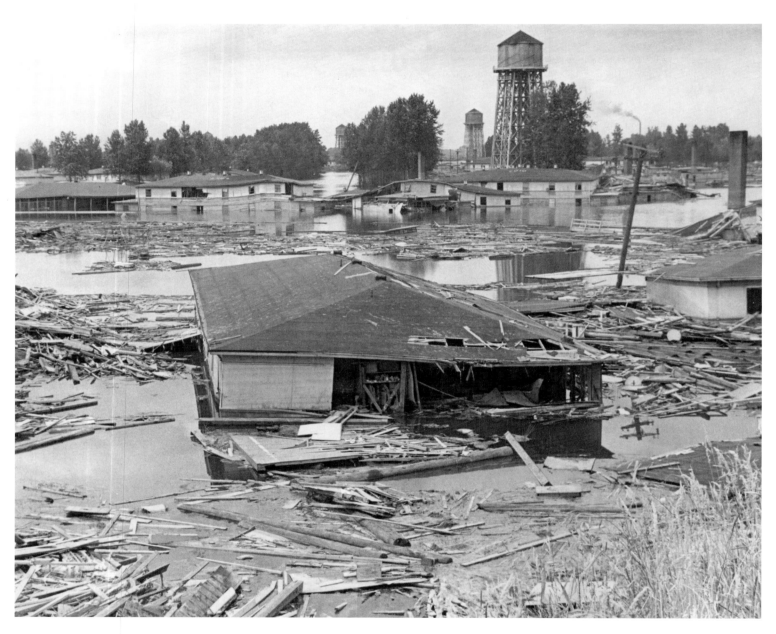

In May 1948, floodwaters of the Columbia River washed out a railroad fill in several places causing the
Vanport community to be inundated with water; apartment houses were ripped from their foundations.
Although there was much devastation, loss of life was minimal.

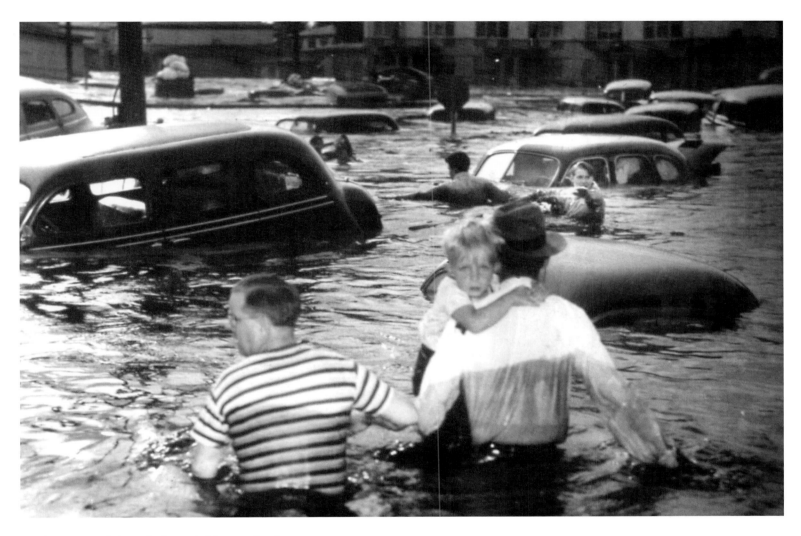

Boy being carried through the 1948 Vanport floodwaters

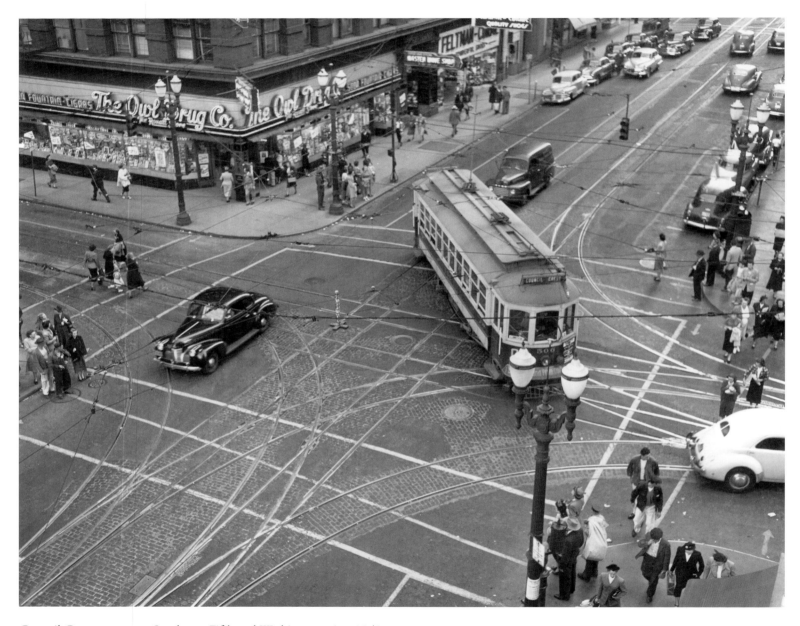

Council Crest streetcar at Southwest Fifth and Washington, circa 1949

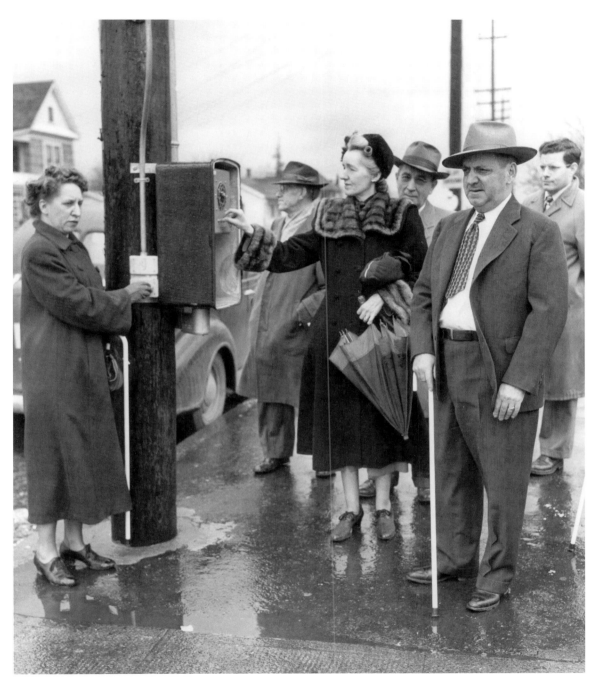

Portland Mayor Dorothy McCullough Lee, center, at a new Blind School crossing signal in March 1950

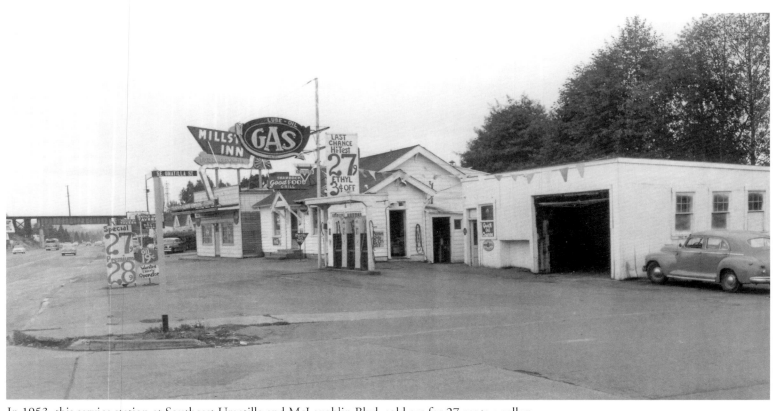

In 1953, this service station at Southeast Umatilla and McLaughlin Blvd. sold gas for 27 cents a gallon and oil for 19 cents a quart. A small sign at the left reads "Wanted: Elderly Operator."

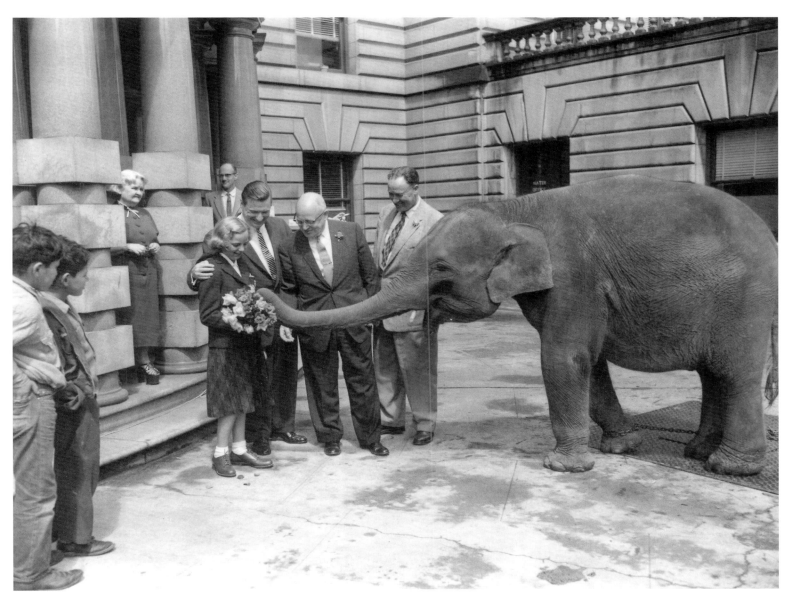

Rosy, a four-year-old elephant from Thailand, was brought to Portland for its zoo. She accepts a bouquet of roses at City Hall on September 26, 1953. Mayor Fred L. Peterson is in the center of the group.

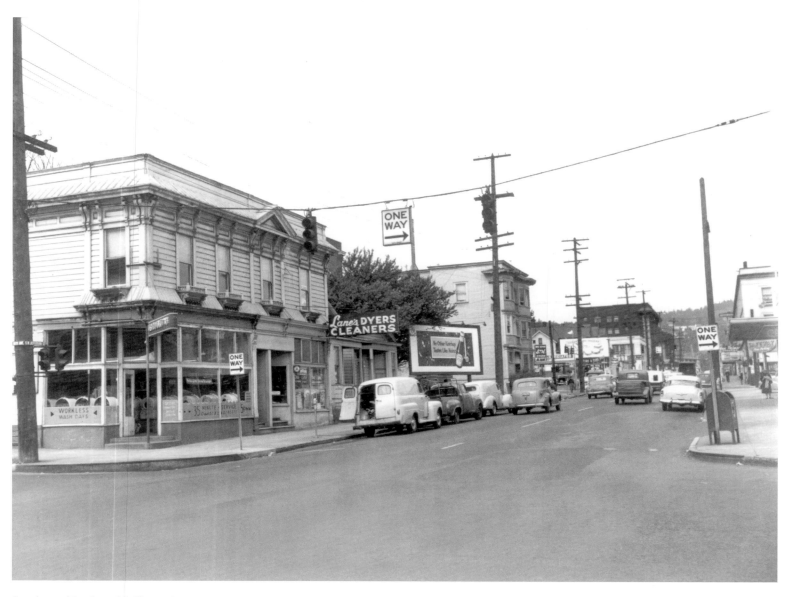

Southwest Tenth and Jefferson in 1953

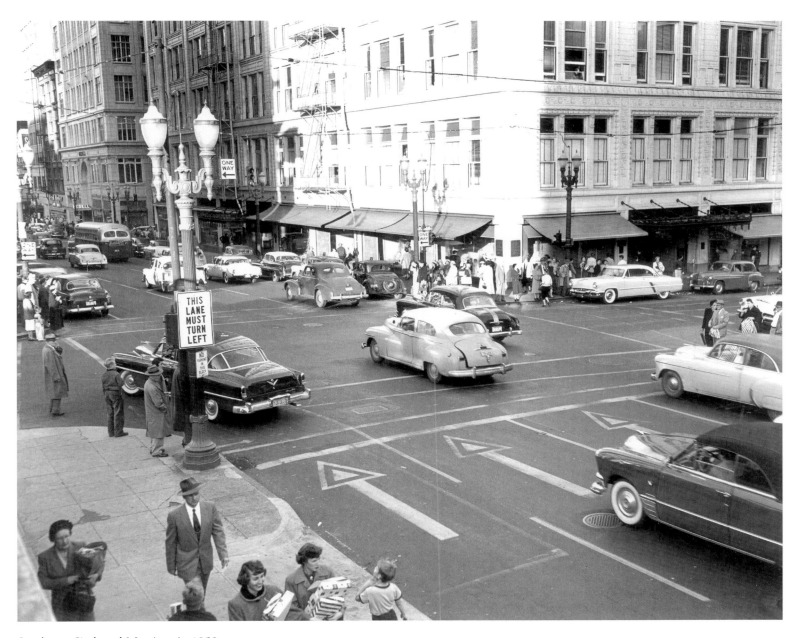

Southwest Sixth and Morrison in 1953

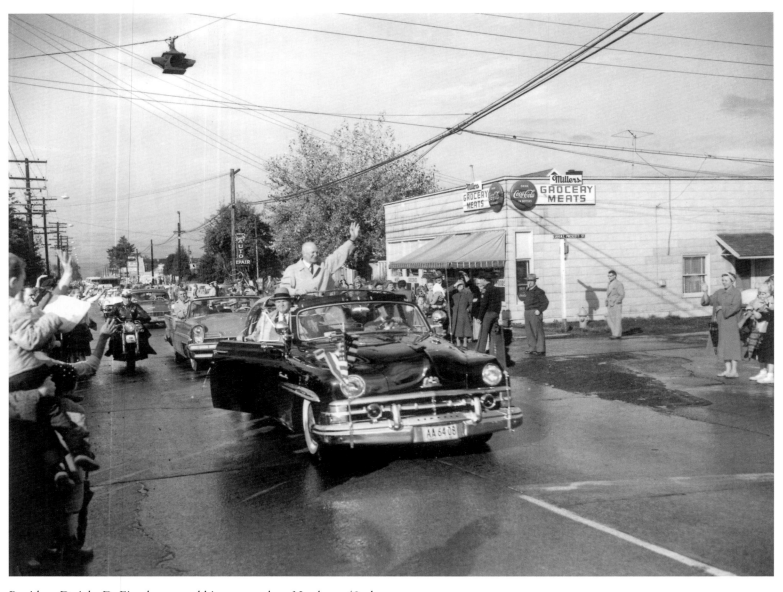

President Dwight D. Eisenhower and his motorcade at Northeast 42nd
and Prescott, a few weeks before the 1956 election

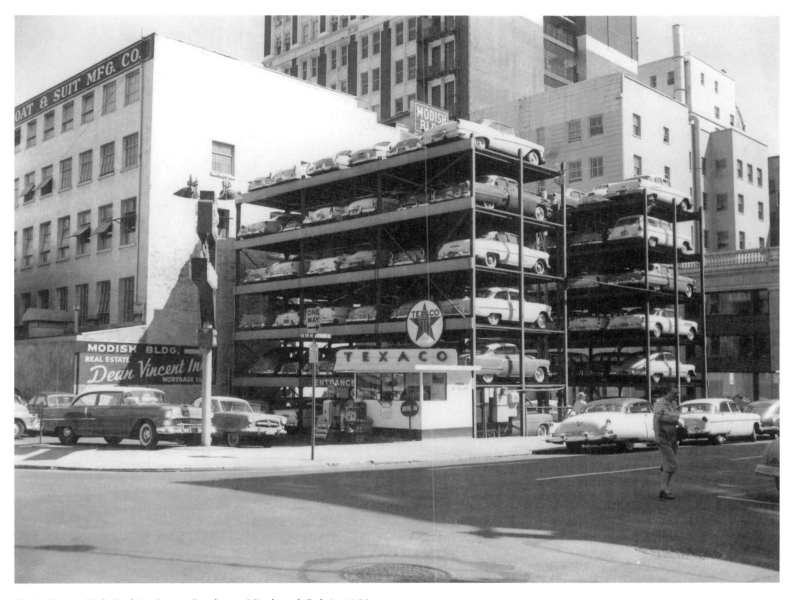

Davis Pigeon Hole Parking Lot at Southwest Ninth and Oak in 1955

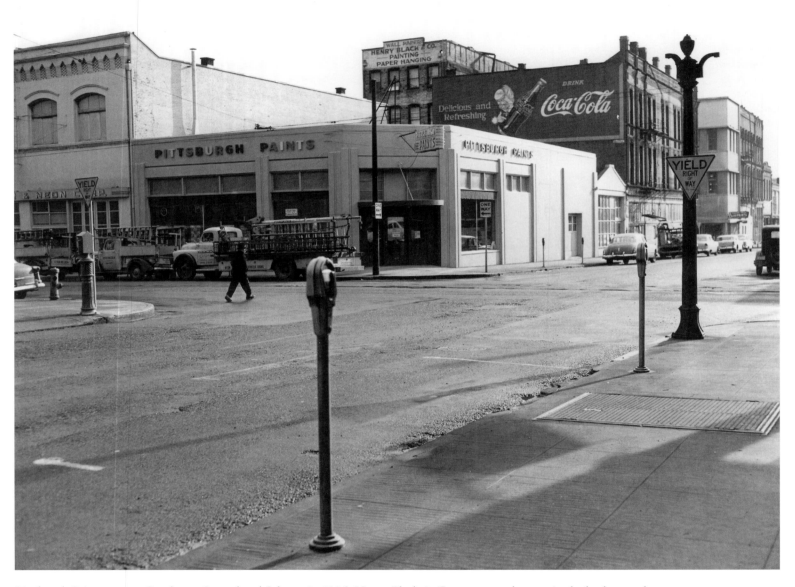

Pittsburgh Paints store at Southwest Second and Salmon in 1956. Henry Black & Company can be seen in the background.

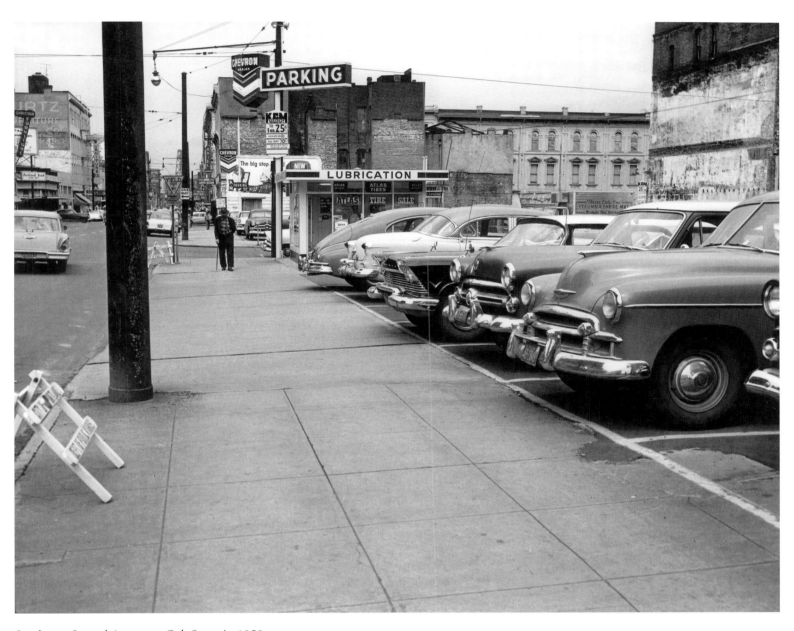

Southwest Second Avenue at Oak Street in 1958

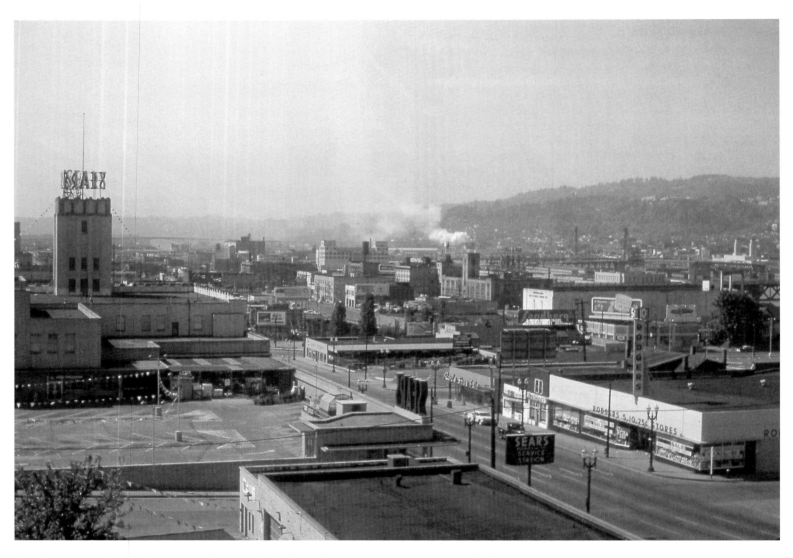

Northeast Union Avenue (Martin Luther King Jr. Boulevard), circa 1958. Note the Sears buildings.

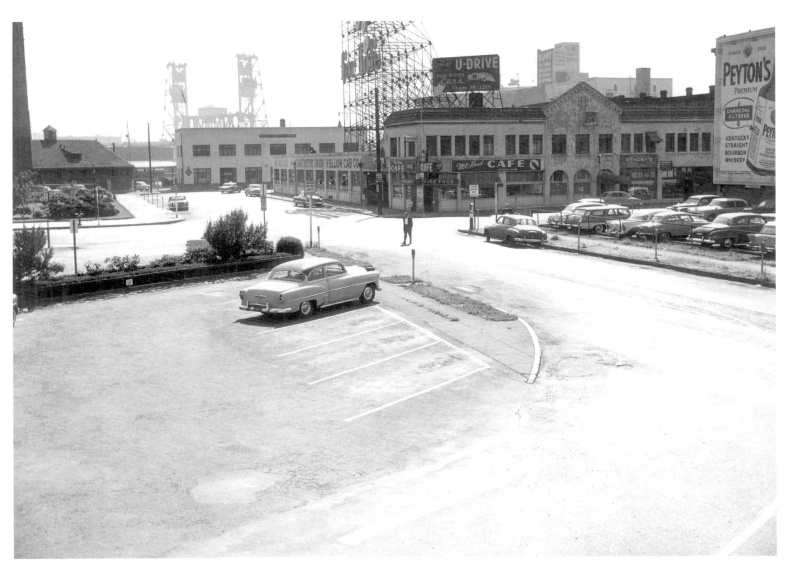

Mt. Hood Cafe and Union Station parking at Northwest Sixth and Irving in 1959

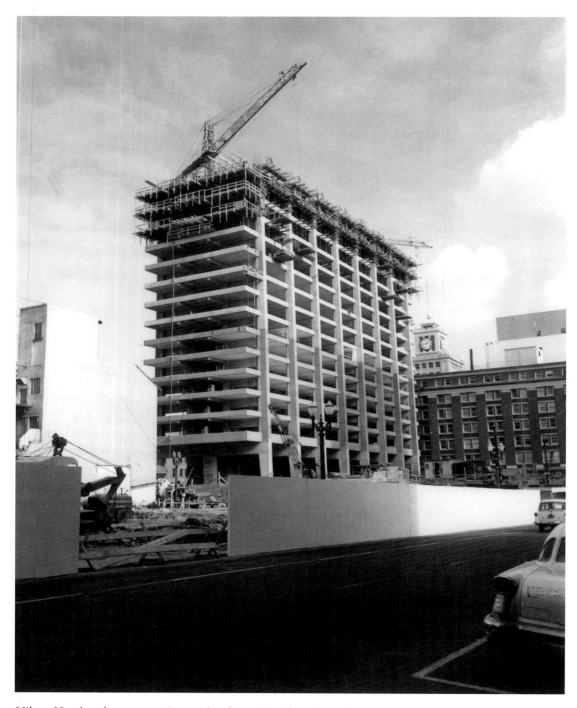

Hilton Hotel under construction on Southwest Broadway in 1962

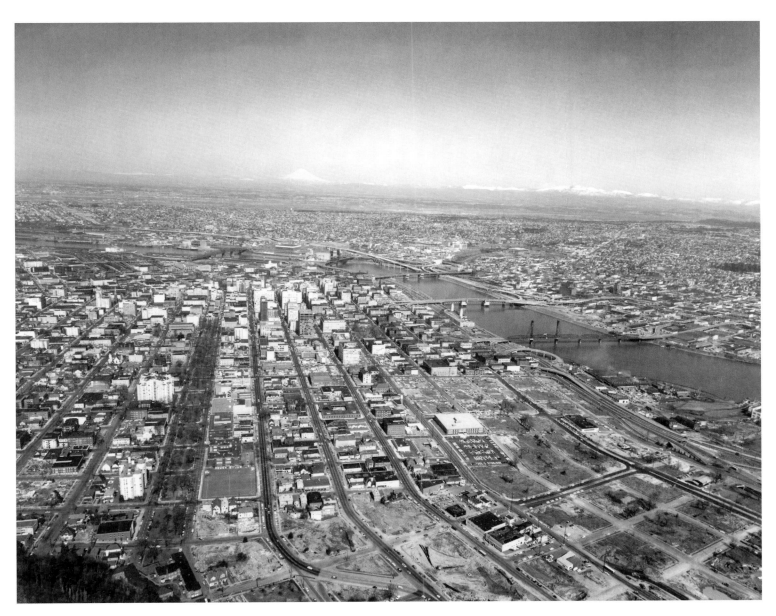

Aerial view of the city in 1964. The South Park Blocks are seen on the left. Urban renewal area is on the right, foreground.

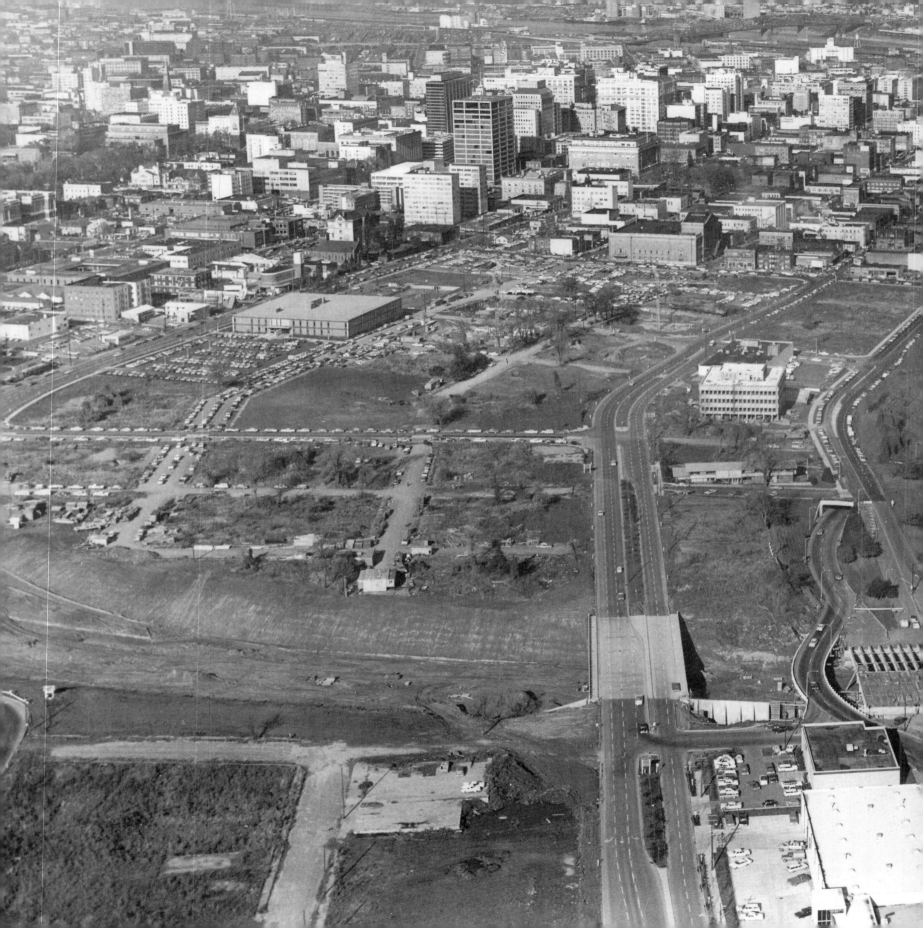

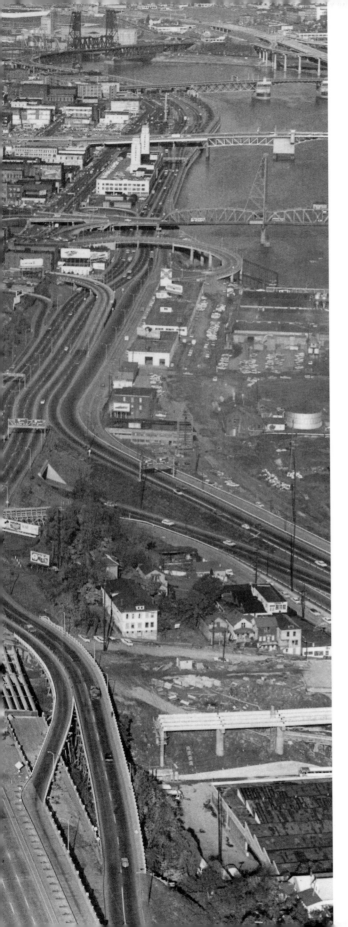

South Auditorium urban renewal and freeway construction in 1963

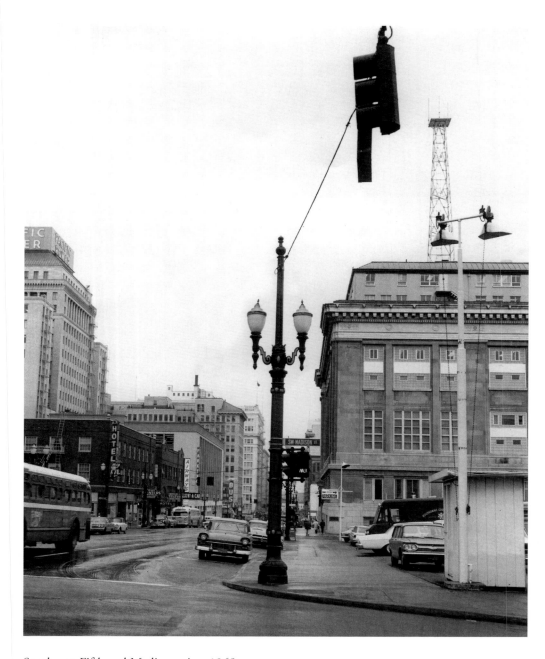

Southwest Fifth and Madison, circa 1965

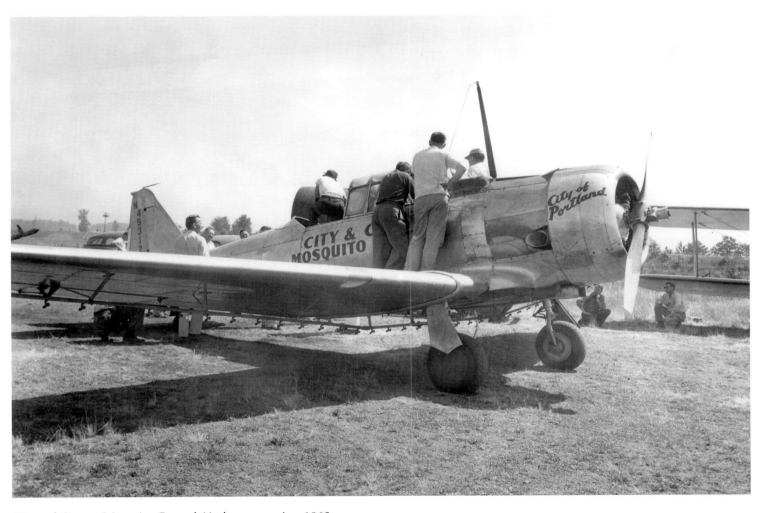

City and County Mosquito Control Airplane crew, circa 1965

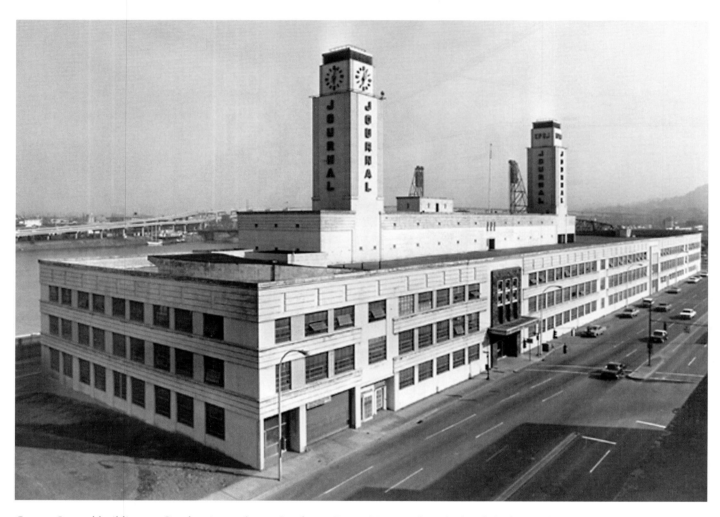

Oregon Journal building on October 31, 1969, on Southwest Front (Naito Parkway), shortly before its demolition

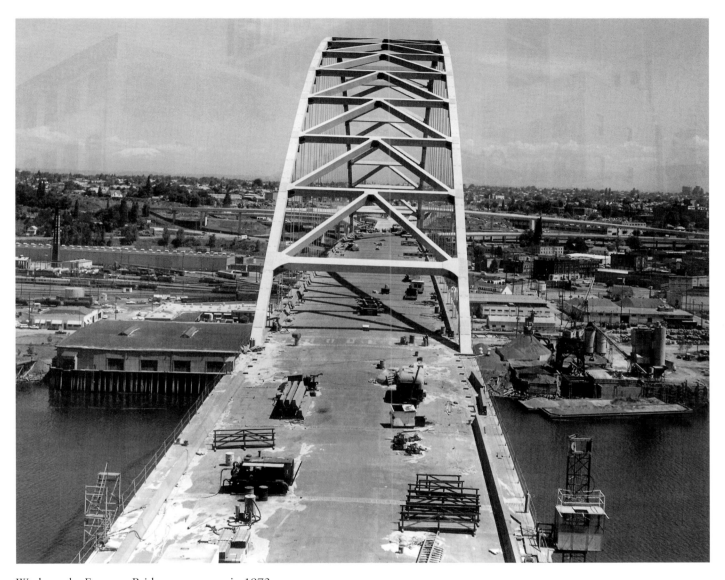

Work on the Fremont Bridge center span in 1972

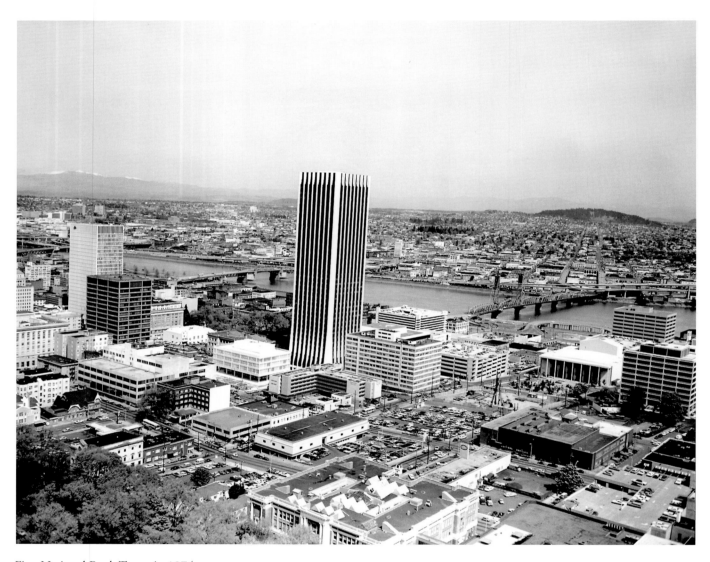

First National Bank Tower in 1974

NOTES ON THE PHOTOGRAPHS

These notes, listed by page number, attempt to include all aspects known of the photographs. Each of the photographs is identified by the page number, photograph's title or description, photographer and collection, archive, and call or box number when applicable. Although every attempt was made to collect all available data, in some cases complete data was unavailable due to the age and condition of some of the photographs and records.

II   FOURTH OF JULY OUTING
      Nelson Photo Archive

VI   PROTECTION COMPANY FIREMEN
      City of Portland Archives
      A2001-083

X   1894 PANORAMIC VIEW OF
      PORTLAND
      City of Portland Archives
      A2004-002.635

2   CAPTAIN R. R. THOMPSON'S
      HOUSE
      Yamhill County Historical Society

3   STUDENTS IN FRONT OF
      CENTRAL SCHOOL
      Mary Couch Robertson Butler
      Collection

4   THE PORTLAND ACADEMY
      Mary Couch Robertson Butler
      Collection

5   FIRST BAPTIST CHURCH
      City of Portland Archives
      A2004-002.636

6   NEW MARKET THEATRE
      Gholston Collection

7   RESIDENCE OF HENRY W.
      CORBETT
      Mary Couch Robertson Butler
      Collection

8   VIEW FROM SEVENTH STREET
      Failing Family Archive

9   PORTLAND POST OFFICE
      Failing Family Archive

10   VIEW OF SIXTH STREET
      Failing Family Archive

11   PORTLAND'S COMBINED
      COURTHOUSE, POST OFFICE,
      AND CUSTOMS HOUSE
      Nelson Photo Archive

12   VIGILANCE HOOK AND LADDER
      City of Portland Archives
      A2001-083

13   PORTLAND POLICE
      Portland Police Historical Society

14   FERRYBOAT CROSSING THE
      WILLAMETTE RIVER
      Nelson Photo Archive

15   PORTLAND HOTEL
      Gholston Collection

16   THE BISHOP SCOTT ACADEMY
      Nelson Photo Archive

17   JUDGE P. A. MARQUAM'S OFFICE
      BUILDING
      Nelson Photo Archive

18   GEM SALOON IN 1890
      Nelson Photo Archive

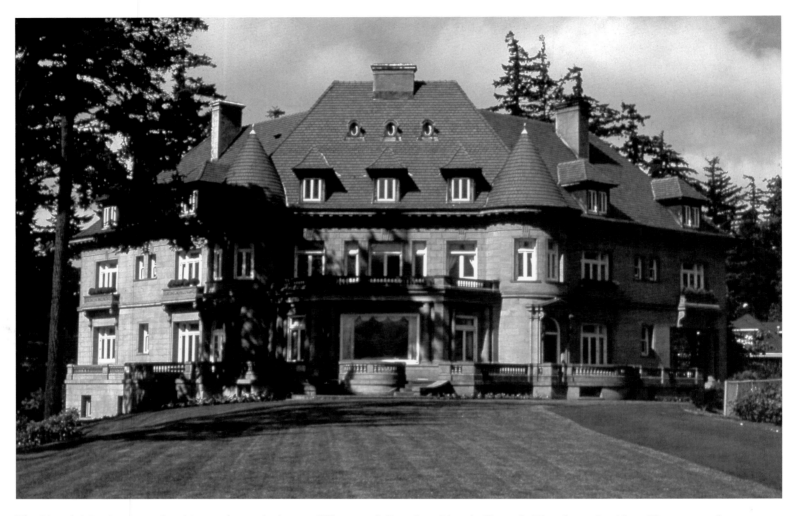

The Pittock Mansion, completed in 1914, was the home of Henry and Georgiana Pittock. Henry L. Pittock was President, Treasurer, and Manager of the Oregonian Publishing Company. Almost lost to redevelopment, a group of concerned citizens led efforts to preserve it, resulting in the City of Portland purchasing the house and surrounding acreage in 1964. Donald R. Nelson photo 1977